INTO THE WILD
WITH A VIRGIN BRIDE

INTO THE WILD
WITH A VIRGIN BRIDE

Best wishes —

Bob Christenson

BOB CHRISTENSON

To order additional copies of this book, contact:
Xlibris Corporation
1-888-795-4274
www.Xlibris.com
Orders@Xlibris.com
76234

CONTENTS

Day 11

For Sue,
who keeps me grounded

British Columbia

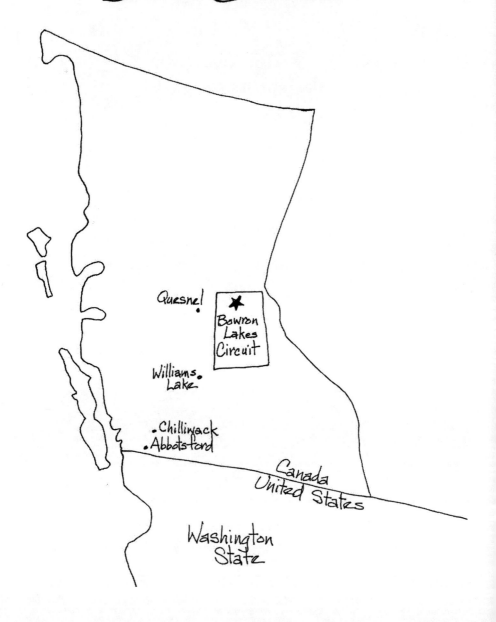

Bowron Lakes Circuit

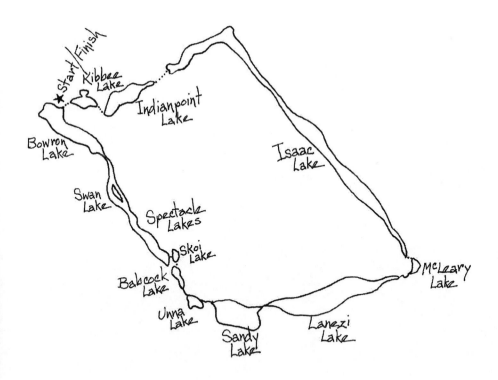

A WOULD-BE MOUNTAIN MAN AND A CITY GIRL

THE WILD

High in the Cariboo Mountains of Canada's British Columbia lies a series of lakes, each with its own personality. Some are shallow, choked with water lilies and other aquatic plant life favored by browsing moose. Some are deep and windswept, fed with mountain streams, home to beaver, mink, and muskrat. Several of the lakes are landlocked, and others are connected by rivers. Some of these rivers rush over deep aquamarine pools, breaking into white water as they carve channels from hilly terrain. Others are murky with the latte-colored flow of glacial runoff. For canoeists, these chocolate streams are especially dangerous because they hide treacherous rocks and corpses of trees torn from banks above.

Early explorers discovered something unique about these lakes. Separated by a high ridge of mountains, the lakes form a rectangle. A traveler can cross overland from one lake to the next, canoe the connecting rivers, and return to his starting point without backtracking. In the first decade of the twentieth century, adventurers began making this trip, marking trails for those to follow.

In 1926, the provincial government proclaimed the area a game reserve. The black bears and grizzlies, which had become increasingly attracted to the supplies carried by these canoeists, gained official protection. Defense against their aggressive raids changed from firing guns to beating tin pans and blowing whistles.

In 1961, the government declared the region a provincial park. Crews built rudimentary campsites and developed the trails. Before long, canoe enthusiasts from around the world began arriving, attracted by the adventure of this seventy-mile challenge. Bowron Lake Provincial Park officially opened for business.

*   *   *

In a fifteen-year period from 1972 to 1987, I traveled the circuit six times. On the first trip, I was accompanied by my twelve-year-old son. Kip and I were novices. Having completed a Red-Cross class in basic canoeing, we traveled to Bowron Lake, rented a canoe, and through a hodgepodge of trial and error successfully completed the circuit.

After three additional trips with other companions, my fifth visit was the ultimate challenge: a solo trip, moving my canoe and gear over the trails and down the lakes and rivers with no help from anyone else and, more importantly, no companionship.

All my life I've been fascinated by stories of the mountain men who crisscrossed the Rockies in search of something that most of them could never have put into words. These men did not seek an experience to share with others. Whatever they sought in the wilderness was best attained in solitude.

The Bowron Lake canoe trip can be crowded even though a reservation system limits the number of people allowed into the park. But somehow for this fifth trip, I had chosen a time when few travelers were on the circuit. For the first few days, I was alone, and for the rest of the trip, I seldom saw more than three or four people on any given day.

It was a time in my life when I needed both solitude and challenge. On cool evenings as I watched the setting sun paint an orange sky, I felt an affinity with a generation of men in a distant past who had traveled and trapped the streams of the Cariboo range. This solo trip was the one that had the greatest impact upon me.

But the trip that proved to be the most fun—the one filled with storms, bears, bloodshed, stealth-attack loons, insomniac porcupines, and naked Germans—was shared with my best friend, my wife Sue.

THE VIRGIN BRIDE

Sue is a city girl. Raised by a single mother, she grew up living in apartments on the east side of Portland, Oregon. Sue learned to swim in the city's park pools. I learned to swim in the Clackamas River.

By the time I was a teenager, my ideal weekend was to hike into the North Fork drainage of the upper Clackamas River, rig my fishing gear, and sneak up on unsuspecting trout.

My campsites were simple: rings of rocks for my cooking fires and cleared spaces for my tarp and sleeping bag. On good days, I cooked trout in my crusty frying pan. On days when the fish were on to me, I ate peanut butter sandwiches.

By the time Sue was a teenager, her ideal weekend was to be first in line for a department store sale with enough time left over for ice cream at a lunch counter and a matinee movie at a downtown theater. The two of us were worlds apart.

But when we married, we each tried to bridge those worlds. I continually met people who claimed my wife as an adopted member of their families. Even counting my most casual acquaintances, I could not begin to equal the number of people who claimed Sue for their own.

Many of these were Italian families with children of marriageable age. Remarkably, most of them decided to marry during the first six months Sue and I were together.

In my new role as an introvert joined in holy matrimony to an extrovert, I began attending weddings. Seemingly every weekend during the wedding season, I attended weddings. I am not a wedding person, but I attended weddings.

And, of course, these Italian families were Catholic. In every case, the parents received their money's worth by opting for the long version of a Catholic wedding. This version is not just long; it's butt-numbing, eyelid-drooping long.

I began to realize why Catholics have so much movement in their services, all that kneeling, standing up, sitting down, rekneeling. If everyone had to stay in a single position for an entire Catholic wedding, they'd need a fleet of wheelchairs to move people into the parking lot.

As for Sue, she readily accepted the challenges of *my* world. She hiked the Clackamas River trail. She climbed to an overlook above Mirror Lake on the slopes of Mt. Hood, awed by the view of a world so far beyond the excitement of Friday Surprise at Meier and Frank's Department Store. She giggled as I drank too much Scotch while preparing goulash in a large blackened pot over the coals of our fire pit on the banks of Timothy Lake. We snuggled under a wool blanket and watched for shooting stars in a sky not dimmed by city lights.

*   *   *

So when I suggested we do the Bowron Lake circuit, Sue was quick to say yes. Too quick. I explained that this was a wilderness trip. Our day hikes, our camping in improved areas—these were not preparation for the Bowron circuit. I emphasized the hardship of carrying backpacks and a canoe over marshy terrain, of being blown off lakes by storms that could last for days, of encountering aggressive bears. However, I made the major mistake of showing Sue a map of Bowron Lake Provincial Park.

The following warning was prominently displayed on the disclaimer all had to sign before setting out on the circuit:

> *Registration is for statistical purposes only. It does not obligate the British Columbia Parks Branch to undertake search operations because a canoeist is late in returning.*

In other words, once out on the circuit, the traveler was on his own. There was no radio contact. There were no access roads. This trip was no "walk in the park." But all Sue saw was the large print on the map: "Bowron Lake Provincial Park."

In her first marriage, Sue had camped with her two boys in Fort Stevens State Park outside Astoria. They reserved a spot for a weekend, choosing a campsite as close as possible to the hot-water showers and five-dollar bundles of firewood. Through the weekend they picked up their rubbish from the mowed grass of the camping areas, rode their bikes on the asphalt paths around the man-made lakes, and bought ice cream from the local grocery outlets. This was "roughing it" in Fort Stevens State Park.

But it was a *state park*. So when Sue saw *provincial park* on the Canadian map, she superimposed *Oregon state park*. She saw mowed grass, asphalt paths. She saw park rangers hovering over campers, ready to leap to their assistance at the first sign of trouble.

Now I must give Sue credit. When I explained this was really a wilderness outing, she understood. At least she *thought* she understood. She understood there'd be no hot showers. She understood she'd have to carry a pack. She understood she'd sleep in a two-man tent and eat freeze-dried food. She understood.

But she *didn't* understand. She had no frame of reference to understand. No matter how hard she tried, *provincial park* subconsciously meant *Oregon state park*. She was a city girl being taken to a Canadian wilderness, a wilderness of wild rivers, windswept lakes, and unpredictable wildlife. A wilderness where charge cards had no meaning, where at any moment Jack London's world became the only reality, the only testament by which survival was measured. She was, in relationship to this Canadian wilderness, a virgin, an offering to the gods of the natural world.

DAY 1

LATE START

We arrived at Bowron Lake around two o'clock on a warm August afternoon, having spent the night in Quesnel, where we had eaten in the local steak house.

"When we finish the circuit, we'll want to be back here for a big rugged steak and a green salad," I said over a plate of Fraser River salmon. Sue looked amused.

"Seriously," I said, stabbing a butter-dripping broccoli spear. "We're going to be so famished for meat and green vegetables, this'll be a place of heaven-sent recuperation."

Sue grinned and shook her head. "Salmon won't do it?"

"No way," I replied, stroking my garlic bread through the sauce on my plate. "If I'm lucky, we'll have some fish. But after two weeks of freeze-dried meals, you'll return here with a proper respect for the basics of red meat."

Sue merely smiled and forked a feta-cushioned bite of tomato into her mouth.

*   *   *

So there we were, unloading the canoe and one hundred pounds of necessities in two backpacks. The food and other items with sweet smells attractive to bears would be carried in one pack. Everything else would be in the second pack. If we found ourselves unable to put both packs into a bear cache, we could take the second pack into our tent with us.

Items with sweet smells? A common error of neophytes in bear country is taking their personal kits into their tents at night. Toothpaste, shampoo, deodorant, scented bug repellent, soap, and cosmetics—these all smell tasty to a bear. People with these items in their tents just might wake up to the presence of a large, furry, and definitely uninvited guest.

Sue would carry the food pack, its weight mercifully lessening each day. I would carry the rest. And, of course, I would carry the canoe. Seventy-five pounds of delicately balanced weight on my shoulders, the kneeling pads, camp shovel, life jackets, and paddles tied in to balance the weight.

Portaging meant three trips over each trail between the lakes and rivers. We would take the canoe over first and then return for the packs. A portage listed as two miles on the map actually involved six miles of hiking, four of those miles carrying heavy loads.

After we had signed in at the Registration Center, I shouldered the canoe, and we were on our way.

WELCOME TO THE CROWD

After a two-mile portage from the park's headquarters, we set out on a short, beautiful paddle to the campground at the far side of Kibbee Lake. Rain had fallen during the portage, but the sun was shining by the time we glided from a small entry creek into the lake itself.

This first lake on the circuit is usually overlooked by people setting out on the trip. Lily-padded with trout rising at sunset, Kibbee Lake is a tiny jewel, surrounded by towering trees and fed by several small streams flowing from beaver ponds higher up the hillsides. However, first-day travelers are so intense at the beginning of the circuit that they overrun this little lake, like hurdlers in track who take the first few hurdles too fast and high before settling into their planned pace.

I had decided we wouldn't make this mistake. We would set up camp early, making this first day relatively easy for Sue. And I would get in some evening fishing.

But as we crossed the lake, I was disappointed to see nine canoes upturned near the takeout point. Kibbee Lake's single campground is small. I was sure there would be no room for us.

Though park regulations normally do not allow large parties to travel the circuit, exceptions are sometimes made. In this case, the exception was for a troop of Canadian Boy Scouts. However, in addition to the scout troop, a group of ten people from Seattle had crowded into the campground. The seven scouts and their scoutmaster had Park permission, but I knew the Seattle people had done what many large groups do on the circuit: register as small groups and then rendezvous after the first portage to make the rest of the trip together.

The problem large groups create for other canoeists was obvious in this first campground. Only so many tent sites are available in each camp. Large groups fill up the spaces, forcing others to move on. Sue and I moved on.

What was supposed to be an easy first day turned into a demanding double-portage race against darkness. The trail from Kibbee Lake to Indianpoint Lake is one and one-half miles long, a tough climb on a planked trail up a marshy hillside until solid ground is reached on a wooded peak. From there the trail drops down the east side of the ridge to the second lake on the circuit.

As we neared Indianpoint, Sue, walking ahead to warn me of roots in the trail that I could not see from under the canoe, suddenly exclaimed, "No, no way! You aren't going to believe this." I tilted the bow of the canoe up so that I could see her standing ahead on the trail.

"What?" I asked. "What do you see?"

"Can't you see them?" she replied in an exasperated voice.

"Babes, I can't see twenty feet in front of me with this thing on my shoulders. And I might point out that it's heavy. So spare me the guessing games. What do you see?"

"Tents, fires, canoes, and more people than I care to count," she answered. "That's what I see."

"Great," I sighed.

"At least they're a happy group," Sue said as she turned and started down the trail.

I pulled the bow of the canoe down again and followed. "They oughta be happy," I groused. "*They* have a place to sleep tonight."

After a couple of staggering steps, I fell into rhythm again.

"Okay," I said. "I give. How do you know?"

"How do I know what?"

"How do you know they're happy?"

"Because they're singing, that's how I know. Can't you hear them?"

I listened, and over the crunching of our feet and my own labored breathing, I *did* hear it. Singing.

"Well, see if you can pick up on the song," I suggested. "Maybe if we come in on the chorus, they'll crowd together and let us stay here tonight."

"I don't think we'll know the song," Sue threw back over her shoulder. "They're singing in German."

*   *   *

By the time we reached the campground, the singing had stopped, but the party was just getting underway. Eighteen twenty-something-year-old Germans, greeted us with friendly waves, some saluting with upraised bottles of beer.

"I can't believe it," I whispered to Sue. "They actually carry beer in their packs."

"*This* from a man who carries Scotch," Sue grinned.

"That's entirely different. Scotch is a *civilized* drink. Besides, I don't carry it in glass."

I was very strict about weight in the packs. All food and clipped cooking instructions were placed in ziplocks. Clothing was kept to the basic minimum. We carried nothing extraneous—except, that is, for paperbacks and Scotch. Those were my allowed luxuries: two paperbacks, a plastic bottle containing thirteen single shots of Scotch, and a tiny plastic wine glass with a removable stem.

Each afternoon between the time camp was set up and dinner, I planned to pour myself a single drink, find a cozy spot on the lakeside, and slowly savor my Scotch while I looked at the mountain ranges across the lake and listened to the sounds of the Canadian wilderness. It would be my downtime and, on some days, my best time.

I must have become a little dreamy-eyed thinking about that single shot of Scotch because I was startled when Sue asked abruptly, "Well, what now? Looks like every campsite is taken."

"We don't have any choice," I answered. "By the time we go back and bring our packs over, the sun'll be setting, and when it gets dark up here, it gets dark fast."

I looked around. "We have to break the Park rules," I said. "Let's find a place where we can set up camp even if it isn't an official site. We won't be able to build a fire, but with the backpack stove we'll have warm food at least."

In just a few steps, Sue asked, "What about over there?" She pointed at an open area on the bank of the lake where some high grass had been matted down.

"Good eyes, Babes. Let's check it out."

I figured it was a place where deer or moose had slept, but what we found was a rectangle area of flattened grass about the size of a pack tent.

"Looks as if someone else had our same problem," I said. "It'll be in the open, and we have to hope for a night without rain or high winds, but it's the best we can do.

"I'll bring the canoe down here to mark the spot as ours. Then we have to hightail it back to Kibbee."

"Hey," Sue replied as we started up the bank toward the canoe, "when it comes to hightailing, I can hightail with the best."

*   *   *

We still had some light when we returned to Indianpoint with our packs, but I figured within an hour we'd be using the flashlights.

We managed to set up the tent and eat our dinner before dark, but by the time I took the packs to the bear cache, the flashlights were necessary. Sue stood below, shining up a light while I struggled to push the Germans' packs together tightly enough to provide room for our food pack. Our other pack would not fit and would have to go into the tent with us. Even so, I silently thanked the Park Service for these bear caches.

On my first two trips around the circuit, there had been no bear caches. Using a system of ropes, campers had to hoist their packs high enough in the air and far enough removed from trees that bears could not reach them from either the ground or nearby trunks. Black bears don't jump, but they climb.

The idea was to string a rope between two trees. A second rope attached to a pack was then thrown over the first rope. Pulling this second rope would lift the pack into the air high enough to suspend it in the desired position halfway between the trees. On paper, the system seemed easy enough.

On that first trip with Kip, I was confident as I prepared to string our first bear cache into the trees. I pulled out my supply of nylon rope. My concern for weight in the packs had driven me to buy the lightest rope possible.

I had not counted, however, on the way nylon rope stretches. Kip and I positioned our cross rope between two trees, tied a rope onto one of our packs, and threw this second rope over the cross rope. Then we pulled . . . and we pulled . . . and we pulled . . . The pack never left the ground. The cross rope simply stretched in a vee until it was barely over our heads. And the inverted apex of the vee pointed directly toward the pack sitting defiantly on the ground.

I'd saved weight, all right. For the rest of the trip, we spent every night with our packs in the tent, acutely attuned to the sounds around us. Each scratchy fir branch, each rustle of weeds, each scampering light-footed squirrel fired our imaginations with thoughts of nose-twitching hungry bears honing in on the succulent smells coming from our tent.

Fortunately, Kip and I had no nocturnal visitors on the trip. Chalk it up to the luck of the innocent. But when I returned to the park for my second trip, I was prepared. I had designed a system comprised of heavy natural-fiber rope, two leather loops and two pulleys. Once I had rigged the gear, I could pull up the pack with an ease that made me the envy of other campers as they struggled with their own ropes and packs.

By the time I made my third trip to the park, the Rangers had provided each campground with a bear-proof system involving no ropes. Two poles stretched between trees, and on the poles crosshatched planks provided a platform for the packs. The lower limbs had been lopped from the trees and the trunks sleeved with tin so that bears could not dig their nails in to climb. And they tried. Oh, how they tried. Every tin sleeve was streaked with long scratches where frustrated bears had clawed for footholds.

A crude heavy ladder made of additional poles and crosshatched planks lay on the ground below each cache. Campers wrestled the ladders upright, struggled to the platforms with their packs, tied the packs firmly into place, and then climbed down and returned the ladders to their original positions on the ground. Failure to complete this final step would probably turn more than one bear into a candidate for Barnum and Bailey.

"Everything okay?" Sue asked as I stepped from the lowest rung of the ladder.

"Fine," I answered. "I had to untie a couple of the Germans' packs and reposition them to find room, but everything is secure. I don't think they'll mind."

"Oh, I don't think they'll mind anything," Sue grinned, motioning toward the Germans, who were laughing and shouting over the popping of pitch-rich wood and the fireflies of sparks spiraling upward from a gigantic fire that served as the gathering place for their party.

"I suspect they'll sleep in tomorrow," I said after we had returned to our chilly fireless camp. "And that'll work well for us."

"Why is that?" Sue asked, sitting in front of the tent to remove her boots.

"We have to get up at first light, eat a quick breakfast of oatmeal and coffee, and get out of here as fast as possible," I answered, sitting beside her to remove my own boots. "If we don't put some distance between ourselves and the Scouts and Germans, we'll be fighting for space the entire trip.

"Besides," I added, crawling into the tent after her, "I don't come up here to travel with people. Present company excepted, of course," I quickly added in response to the look she gave me.

"Of course," she smiled.

We slipped into our sleeping bags, and I arranged the flashlight hanging from a strap above us. I handed her the paperback on which she had claimed dibs when we packed.

"Babes," I began, "I'm sorry this first day was so hard. From now on we'll make camp in plenty of time to relax and enjoy our evenings."

"Are you kidding?" she laughed. "I'm having a ball. I couldn't have a better time." Nevertheless, I noticed as she said this, she was rubbing her shoulder where the pack straps had cut in.

Sue has large turquoise eyes. After twenty-four years together, I still find myself marveling at those eyes. And even in the harsh glare of the flashlight, I found myself drawn to them.

"Well," I said, "just a few pages of reading and then to sleep. We have to get up early and get ahead of this crowd."

If I had known as I looked into her completely trusting, innocent face what that face would look like by the next afternoon—bruised, swollen, and bloodied—I've have said instead, "Let's sleep in, eat a leisurely pancake breakfast, and backtrack our way out of here."

Arrival at Bowron Lake

Portaging

DAY 2

LOONS AND NAKED GERMANS

We crawled from the tent into a cold, damp camp the next morning. The sky was overcast, and a hazy mist rose from the lake. The high grass around our tent was weighed down with heavy dew.

"Did you hear that weird sound last night?" Sue asked, hunched to preserve body heat, her hands around a cup of hot coffee.

"Yeah, I heard lots of weird sounds," I answered. "I thought the Germans were never going to sleep."

"No, not them. Their sounds were fun. No, I mean long after things quieted down. Probably three or four this morning. A weird kind of screeching, wailing sound. It happened several times."

"Oh," I replied. "You mean something like *BIDILLITLITLUP!*"

"Shh!" Sue hissed, her finger to her lips. "You'll wake the Germans."

Then she added, giggling, "But that was it! That was *exactly* it! Can you do it again, only softly this time?"

"No, if I do it softly, it'll sound like a turkey."

"What's it supposed to sound like?"

"A loon."

"A loon? You mean like something from Looney Tunes?"

"Well," I answered, "that's probably where we get the word *loony*. You know, to act crazy like a loon."

"*Are* they crazy?"

"Not really. They just do some funny things."

"Like what?"

"Well, for example, most waterbirds land by pushing their feet out and kind of water-skiing to a stop. Loons don't use their feet. They just crash-land on their bellies."

"What else?" Sue asked, laughing.

"Taking off is even more of an adventure," I grinned. "They get going by flapping their wings and actually running along the surface. And they need a good runway, sometimes up to three hundred yards to get off the water."

"You're kidding! Three hundred yards! The length of three football fields?"

"Exactly. But once in the air they can really move. Up to sixty miles an hour, in fact. And they are great swimmers, especially underwater. They can dive deep and stay under for an amazing length of time."

"Do they always sound crazy like that one last night?" Sue asked, holding her cup against her cheek for the heat.

"Actually they have several calls. What we heard was the sound they make when they feel threatened or are doing a little threatening of their own. They're territorial, and that's the sound they make when they don't like new neighbors."

"So we're invading someone's territory?"

"Babes, when we come up here, we are *constantly* invading someone's territory. But I don't think we were the problem last night. He sounded quite a ways out on the lake.

"However, on one of my trips, I was *obviously* the problem. A pair of loons dive-bombed my tent several times, screeching just like that one last night. I figured they had a nest nearby."

"I really like it when you get into your teacher mode," Sue grinned, moving closer to me. "What other sounds do they make?"

"Well, the neatest is a kind of soft, lonely wail. I hope you hear that one while we're here. It's a late-evening call, supposedly used to make contact with a mate or family member. And it's really pretty. It's kind of *sad* but nice."

"Can you do it?"

"No," I replied, shaking my head. "It's too romantic for me. I can do only the threatening, macho calls."

"Well, macho man," she laughed, getting to her feet, "if we don't start breaking down this camp, we'll have defeated the purpose for getting up so early."

"Right," I replied, handing her my cup. "You rinse out the dishes, and I'll work in the tent, rolling the sleeping bags."

*   *   *

A few minutes later, Sue pulled back the flap of the tent. "You might want to see this," she said, leaning in.

Puzzled, I stuck my head out the tent and found myself eye level with a pair of hiking boots passing by. Higher up was a pair of hairy legs. Higher still was a very naked German, towel over his shoulder, heading for the lake. In tow were several others—both sexes of other—also wearing hiking boots or tennis shoes and nothing else.

"Thought you might enjoy this," Sue whispered, leaning close, "student of nature that you are."

"Whew," I replied. "I don't think they realize how cold that lake is. Maybe," I continued, my eyes fastened on an especially lithe Alpine nymph striding by, "maybe I'd better go down there and watch out for them. Heart attack and all that you know."

"'Watch *out* for them, or simply *watch* them?" Sue grinned.

"Well, I've always been a good Samaritan, and this might be my chance to save lives."

"Sure," Sue replied. "Mouth-to-mouth and all that."

"Exactly. I would never forgive myself if one of those girls died because I wasn't there."

"But what if it's one of the guys?"

"Well," I replied after a moment's thought, "he couldn't have found a nicer place to die."

"Get back to work, macho man," Sue commanded.

"Right," I laughed, ducking back into the tent.

*　　*　　*

By the time we loaded the canoe and shoved off into the lake, the mist had lifted, and the sun was breaking through the clouds. Promise of a good day hung in the air.

We had barely found our rhythm when I suddenly blurted, "There's one right there."

"There's one what?" Sue replied, lifting her paddle.

"A loon. There's one right over there."

"Where?" she asked, looking around.

"Right over there," I said, pointing to the far side of the lake. "See that place where the bank has caved in . . . where that dead tree is sticking out of the water?"

"Okay," Sue answered, nodding.

"Look just to the right of the tree and closer to us."

"No," she began, "I don't see . . . Wait. There it is. I see it."

"That's a loon," I said.

"Can we get closer?"

"Maybe. Better let me do it. We need to be really quiet."

The most beautiful thing about a canoe is its silence. No sputtering motor. No stinking gas fumes. A canoe on a glassy surface is a graceful, gliding, quiet work of art.

We were within twenty feet of the loon when I brought us to a stop.

Sue watched the bird resting nonchalantly on the surface of the lake. "He looks a little like Daffy Duck," she whispered.

"A little," I agreed. "It's the white band around his neck."

"Can we get even closer?"

"We can try, but we'll be pushing our luck," I answered, dipping my paddle into the lake.

"If he sees us, will he make one of those long-range takeoffs?" Sue whispered.

"No, when they're startled, they dive underwat . . ."

Plop. It was gone.

We waited.

"He's been under quite a while," Sue said. "Think he's okay?"

"Give him time," I answered. "He'll come up somewhere. Might be quite a ways from here, though."

Suddenly the water beside the canoe exploded. *BIDILLITLITLUP!* The loon, neck stretched, bill wide open, screeched at us, wings beating a boiling froth on the surface of the lake.

Both of us threw our arms into the air, pulling away from screeching bird. Two paddlers suddenly lunging to the same side of a canoe is not a desirable move under any circumstances. By the time we had brought the violent rocking under control, the loon was gone.

On our knees, hands gripping the gunnels, we knelt is silence.

Sue turned, eyes wide, and pointed wordlessly at her paddle floating by. I leaned over and snatched it.

Handing the paddle to her, I asked, "Well, was that close enough?"

She began to giggle and then burst into laughter. Her infectiousness sucked me in, and the lake soon echoed with a combination of her high-pitched shrieks and my deeper roars.

When we could finally look at each other without starting over, Sue, tears streaking her face, remarked, "The Germans probably think we've gone loony." That set us off again until we both huddled in the canoe, worn out from this shared moment of convulsed hysteria.

"Speaking of the Germans," I began. "Maybe we should, uh, . . ." I motioned with my head down the lake.

"Right," Sue answered.

We swung the canoe around and began to paddle east into a bright, warming sun. "Hey," Sue said over her shoulder. "Quite a morning, huh? Naked Germans . . . attack loons. Think the day'll hold any more surprises for us?"

"Up here the possibility of surprise lies around every corner," I answered.

"I hope so," she laughed. "I love these surprises."

I watched her lean into her stroke and pick up the pace. *This is great,* I thought to myself. *She's really having fun.*

But the fun was going to stop with the next surprise.

SIGNPOSTS AND MOOSE

Indianpoint is one of my favorite lakes on the Bowron circuit. On a good day its color ranges from turquoise to jade. And this was a good day.

The surface was glass smooth, mirroring a blue sky cottoned with clouds. We glided into this reflection, marring it with the vee our canoe left behind. Paddling under such conditions is effortless and transcending. Sue was experiencing canoeing at its best.

But conditions change fast in the Cariboo Mountains. A mile from the end of the lake, I felt a breeze stroke my back and watched it push ripples down the water ahead of us. In just a few minutes, dark clouds appeared over the jagged ridge above the timberline. We were in for more rain.

*   *   *

The east end of Indianpoint presents special challenges for the canoeist. The takeout point is hidden behind a promontory pushing out from a marshy inlet. Paddlers must maneuver along a winding channel through a murky swamp smothered by water lilies. Broken tree trunks and limbs jut from the water, warning of hidden debris below.

The Park Service had marked the channel with squares of orange paint on posts. But I knew from past experience that the posts were easy to miss. As we entered the swamp, I warned Sue to watch for them.

"Orange posts," she replied. "Those should be easy to spot."

"Not orange *posts*," I corrected her. "Orange squares *on* the posts."

"Why didn't they paint the whole posts orange? They'd be easier to see."

"Because this is the Bowron Lake circuit, not I-5. Just look for orange squares."

*　　*　　*

We were about halfway through the marsh when Sue suddenly pointed to the left, exclaiming, "Look! Look over there!" A moose, belly-deep in the water, stood sideways to us, its head turned in our direction. Water dripped from its ears and face. Bits of green vegetation, just torn from below the swamp's surface, hung from its mouth.

"That's so neat," Sue whispered. "Too bad we're stuck in this channel. I'd like to get closer."

"Not too bad at all," I replied. "We're close enough."

"You aren't afraid of *that*, are you? It isn't even a male. See, no horns. Doesn't look any more dangerous to me than a dairy cow."

"Really?" I answered. "Well, if we were closer, you'd see that *dairy cow* is probably six-foot tall at the shoulder and outweighs you by seven hundred pounds. Besides, you're missing something. I pointed up the bank. There standing in the same profile with the same blank stare was an exact miniature of the moose in the water.

"Ooh," Sue cooed, "a baby."

"Just another reason to keep our distance," I said.

"Sometimes you're such a killjoy," Sue replied. "Afraid of a moose. What's it going to do, swim out here and attack us?"

"You've heard the expression 'Hell hath no fury like a woman scorned'? Well, it should be 'Hell hath no fury like a wild animal that thinks its offspring is being threatened.' Unless you want that moose climbing right into this canoe with us, we keep our distance."

In answer to Sue's silent look, I added, "Number-one rule in the wilderness: Never, and I mean *never*, approach an animal with its young nearby."

Sue gave me another of her long silent looks and then pointed to the black clouds overhead. "Shouldn't we be getting on? I don't want to miss any of your precious orange squares in a rainstorm."

TO STITCH OR NOT TO STITCH

The small campground on the east side of Indianpoint is the only ugly campsite on the circuit. A slick muddy bank leads up to the camp with its two fire pits close together near the bear cache. It's the only campground that doesn't look out over a lake. Instead it's located at the edge of the marsh. I can only imagine the swarm of mosquitoes rising from that water at night.

"This place is icky," Sue said, looking around.

"*Icky* isn't the word that first comes to my mind, but I'll take it. Icky or not, we should eat lunch here before portaging over to Isaac." I nodded to the trail going up through the woods. "It isn't raining yet, but it's gonna pretty soon. We don't want to be driven to shelter under the trees." No-see-ums and deep-biting horseflies swarm along the circuit's trails, especially attracted to the salt of human sweat. The rule is heavy application of repellent and short rest periods. The trails are not good choices for lunch breaks.

"Okay," Sue answered. "But I really don't like this place. It gives me the creeps. I have a bad feeling about it."

"Well, let's grab a quick sandwich then and get out of here."

*   *   *

After our hurried lunch, I pulled plastic trash bags over our packs to protect them from the rain and stowed them on the bear cache. Then I shouldered the canoe, and with Sue leading the way, we set out for Isaac Lake, the largest lake on the circuit.

Up one side of a ridge and down the other, this portage is short, only a half mile, the final hundred yards on a planked walkway over another marshy area. The rain had begun by the time we overturned the canoe at the lake's first campsite. We immediately started our return trip to pick up the packs.

*   *   *

The Indianpoint camp was mucky by the time we arrived. Rain drizzled through the trees, and I hurried to prop the heavy ladder against the bear cache. I climbed to the top and brushed a puddle of rainwater from the trash bag covering the pack nearest me. Then I grasped the top bar of the fifty-pound pack through the plastic bag and pulled it from the cache.

What I did not realize was that Sue, who at first had taken refuge from the rain by moving back under the trees, had then decided to help me. She had moved to the foot of the slippery ladder and was holding it steady, looking down to keep the rain out of her face.

When I felt the slick plastic slipping through my fingers, I made a grab for a deeper grip but could not hang on. I grabbed again for the falling pack, looked down and saw Sue below. "*Watch out!*" I yelled, causing her to look up just as the pack hit her squarely in the face and drove her into the mud of the campground that had filled her with such a sense of foreboding.

*   *   *

By the time I reached Sue, she was on her knees, struggling to stand up.

"Stay down," I said, kneeling in front of her.

"I'm okay," she replied.

"Just sit still and let me see," I said, putting my hands on her shoulders. Blood oozed from two cuts, one on the right side of her nose and the other near her right eye.

I described the cuts to her as I took off my jacket and tugged the sleeve of my shirt over my palm. I began dabbing at the wounds. Blood from the cut on her nose had reached her upper lip. I cupped her chin and lifted her head. "Try to keep your head back," I said, hoping to keep the blood out of her mouth.

Sue's eyes rolled skyward. "Well, one good thing," she said.

"What's that?" I asked, moving from one cut to the other in an attempt to stay ahead of the blood.

"It quit raining."

"Be quiet. I don't have time for weather reports."

She giggled and dropped her head as I moved to change shirtsleeves, the left one soggy with blood. When she looked up again, blood trickled down her forehead.

"What?" she asked, alarmed at what she saw in my face.

I pushed her bangs back from her hairline. The hair was matted with blood. When I lifted it with a sweeping motion, the blood that had been held back by hair began to run down her face.

Before I could stop it, blood dripped into one eye. Her face whitened as she instinctively swiped at the eye and came away with a red-streaked palm.

I took her head in both hands and pulled it down. The front third of her hair was filled with blood. The matted hair prevented me from seeing the wound.

I stood up, stripped off my shirt, and pulled my T-shirt over my head. Pressing the T-shirt against the top of her head in an attempt to stanch the flow, I said softly, as much to comfort myself as Sue, "Scalp wounds are notorious bleeders. This probably isn't as bad as it looks."

"Well, I can't see how bad it looks," she replied, "but I doubt I'm ready for company."

"What are you talking about?"

"I just heard a canoe scrape on the rocks," she answered.

I looked down to the canoe takeout point. Ankle-deep in water by the bow of his canoe stood the Canadian scoutmaster. At the stern was one of his scouts, and turning the last bend of the channel were two more of their canoes.

"Need some help?" the scoutmaster called, pulling the canoe up the bank.

In answer, I nodded, lifting my bloody T-shirt. The young scout in the stern had just begun to work his way forward in the canoe. But the sight of a bare-chested man hovering over a woman and holding a bloody shirt caused him to sit back down. His eyes widened at what must have looked like a scene from the latest slasher movie.

*   *   *

The scouts, in keeping with their motto, were well prepared for emergencies. While I had a small medicine kit that I had carried unopened for years, they had a kit the size of a fishing-tackle box. Using a couple of cotton compresses, we managed to stop the bleeding. However, Sue's hair was so matted with blood that we had difficulty assessing the extent of her injury.

"I'd say it's a cut at least three or four inches long," the scoutmaster said, peering into the matted hair. "Hard to tell how deep it is. I think we're going to have to cut some hair away."

I knelt in front of Sue. "I don't think we have any choice, Babes. We have to get a closer look."

"Do what you have to do," she replied. "But as long as you're there, I'd like the sides feathered as well."

"What'll we use?" I asked the scoutmaster, straightening up. All I have is this." I patted my hunting knife in the scabbard on my belt.

"We have some tape scissors," he answered, rummaging in his kit. "Yup," he continued, holding up the scissors, "these should do it."

*　　*　　*

I spent a shaky ten minutes cutting Sue's hair. Beginning at her hairline, I cut away a swath of blood-soaked hair approximately two to three inches wide. Working inward, I clipped the hair to the cut and then scissored along both sides of it until we could clearly see the wound in its entirety.

The scoutmaster had been right. The cut was about three inches long. It began a couple of inches in from her hairline and ended near the top of her head. When I had finished cutting, Sue had a kind of miniature reverse Mohawk. I had left the hair as long as I could, approximately one half to one inch in length, but with the long hair on the sides, she looked like someone who had experienced a disastrous encounter with a weed eater.

"It's kinda cute, Babes," I ventured, trying to make her feel better. Inwardly, however, I was thankful that we carried no mirrors.

"You're a terrible liar," she replied. "You really are."

Then she added, "Do we have any aspirin?"

"We do," the scoutmaster answered, "and I'm sure you need one, but aspirin is a blood-thinner. If you can, it'd be better if you didn't take one right now."

"Why?" Sue asked. "You said the bleeding had stopped."

"It has," he answered, "but we may have to start it up again."

He turned to me. "Could we talk over there?" He motioned with his head away from Sue. We made our way through the semicircle of scouts, who had been watching all this in the kind of reverent hush usually associated with funeral services.

"We need to close the wound," he said in a low voice. "I think it needs sutures. We don't have anything that sophisticated in *our* kit. How about you?"

"Nothing like that," I answered. "But I do . . . No, that's crazy," I said, shaking my head.

"What?" he asked.

"Well, I do have a sewing kit, you know, for sewing on buttons or fixing rips in sleeping bags or clothing. But that's regular needles and thread. That's not the stuff doctors use."

He looked at me for a long moment. Finally he said, "That may have to do. Let's take another look."

*　　*　　*

"You're going to *what*!" Sue exclaimed.

"Not for sure," I answered, stepping backward. "We just need to take another look. But if it's too bad, we have to close it, or it'll be infected before we get back to Bowron."

"That's why you wouldn't give me an aspirin, isn't it?" Sue said to the scoutmaster. "You're planning to punch needle holes in my scalp."

"No, if it comes to sewing, I'd prefer your husband do that."

"Are you kidding? He doesn't sew. When I first met him, he hemmed pants with a stapler. I'd rather have him *staple* my head. At least he'd have a better chance of getting it right."

"Well, let's take another look," he suggested, and we leaned over Sue's head once again.

"It's pretty deep," he whispered, as if Sue weren't right there. "Also, it's a little jagged. I think we do need to close it."

"What about sterilization?" I whispered back. "We can use matches for the needle, but what do we do about the thread?"

"Alcohol swabs would do it, but one of the boys cut his finger in the last campground, and we used what we had in our kit. How about you?"

"No, if I had any, they dried up years ago."

"Well, alcohol is the answer. We, of course, don't carry any liquor. Any chance you do?"

Oh, no, I thought to myself, *my Scotch*!

I heard Sue giggle, and I stepped back to look at her. "What are you snickering about?" I asked.

"Because I know *exactly* what is going through your mind right now. Okay, what's it going to be, your wife or your Scotch?"

"Scotch?" the scoutmaster asked. "You carry Scotch? Perfect. We can sterilize the thread, and perhaps," he added in a lowered voice, glancing at the scouts, "the three of us can share a little congratulatory nip after this bloody business is over with."

*　　*　　*

I can't do this, I thought to myself, looking at the sewing kit in my hand.

The campground seemed so quiet with the scouts gone. To save Sue the embarrassment of having seven curious boys watch what she was about to endure, the scoutmaster had instructed them to carry their canoes over the trail to Isaac Lake. The older boys had responded well, taking charge of the move, but a younger, chubby scout had protested, saying he wanted to stay and "see the lady get her head sewed up."

I looked over at Sue, holding the last clean compress to her wound as she sat on a log overlooking the marshy takeout point below. She looked abandoned. I needed to go to her, but the prospect of what I had to do there held me back.

The clouds had passed, and steam rose from the muddy ground as the campground warmed in sunlight. The scoutmaster, who had accompanied his charges partway into the woods, emerged from the trees and approached me.

I looked down at the sewing kit again. When I heard his footsteps stop and felt his shadow fall across me, I said once more—only aloud this time—"I can't do this."

"I think you have to," he replied. "Even if you backtrack out of here, it'll take you two days. Two days with that cut open could really have serious consequences. Infection . . . bad scarring . . . serious consequences. No," he continued, "it has to be closed."

I looked up. "I've been thinking," I began. "What if we use the scissors and some tape to make some butterfly bandages?"

"Well, you don't have to make any," he replied. "We have butterflies in our kit."

"What! Why didn't you say so?"

"Because they won't work. You can't get tape to stick to hair."

"There's an alternative," I answered.

"What?"

"We remove the hair."

His eyes wandered over my two-day beard. "You carry a razor?" he asked.

"No, but I think I can do it with the scissors."

"I don't think so," he replied. "You'll have to get right down to the scalp to get the tape to stick. I don't think you can do that with scissors."

"It's worth a try," I answered. "If it doesn't work, we can always go back to plan one."

"Yeah," he said, "but then you'll have cut off her hair and *still* have to stitch her up."

"I think it's worth a try," I repeated. "I'm going to run it past her."

"Okay," he said, glancing over at Sue. "But I'm glad it's you, not me."

*   *   *

"Well," Sue said as we walked toward her, "have you two finally worked up the courage to do this?"

When neither of us answered, she asked, "Why are you looking at me like that? I swear if I were a horse, you'd just shoot me and get it over with."

"Babes," I began, kneeling in front of her, "I need to ask you something."

"Okay," she replied, "so ask me."

"What would you rather have—stitches or a partially bald head?"

"Is this a trick question?"

"Huh-uh," I answered. And then I began to explain the options.

*   *   *

When I stopped talking, Sue sat quietly for a moment. Then she said, "Let's see if I have this right. You're going to cut off my hair—right down to the scalp, is it? *Or* you're going to use a needle and thread to stitch me up. Don't you have to cut off some more hair even to do that?"

"Yeah, but not as much. The butterflies are two inches long. We'd have to cut the hair back at least a couple of inches on each side of the cut in order for the tape to stick. If we sew it, we just need to take away a half inch or so."

"Do you really think I even have to consider this?" she replied. "A little injury to my vanity *or* your left-handed embroidery on my scalp? Those are my choices? Lose the hair," she concluded. "I can't believe you even bothered to ask."

*   *   *

Losing the hair proved to be even more difficult than the scoutmaster had thought. While I cut, he stood by with several strips of tape, testing to see if they would stick. I had managed to trim a five-inch-wide semicircle to a field of fuzz before he finally announced, "I think we got it. Look at this." He tugged the strip he had last applied. It stuck.

"Try another one just to be sure," I responded. He moved to the other side of the cut and applied a second strip. It stuck.

"Good," I said. "Let's do it."

"Ouch!" Sue yelped as he pulled off one of the strips, bringing up a fuzz-covered piece of tape.

"Sorry," he said. Then he leaned over to me and whispered, "But you know what? If we have trouble, we might get the fuzz off this way," pointing to the tape.

"I *heard* that," Sue warned.

*   *   *

We had just applied the last butterfly when the scouts returned. "Did you do it? Did you sew up the lady's head?" the chubby scout asked as he hurried toward us.

"We're all done here, Jimmy," the scoutmaster responded, holding up his hand. "Nothing to see. You and the others start getting the packs ready. We'll be heading out in just a few minutes."

He turned back to Sue. "It looks good," he said. "Your husband did a good job. You'll need to keep it covered for several days to keep it clean and dry. Just keep a hat on it, that's all."

Sue looked up at me. "Of course, he did a good job. Was there ever any doubt?"

The scoutmaster looked over his shoulder at the scouts helping each other with their backpacks. "I'm going to check on the boys," he said. "I'll be right back."

After he left, I said to Sue, "Thanks for the vote of confidence."

"Well, I knew you'd take care of me," she smiled. "But there is one thing."

"What's that?"

"I don't *have* a hat."

"I *know* you don't have a hat. When I told you to bring one, you said you didn't wear hats. Remember? You would be fine with the hood on your jacket. You wouldn't listen to me."

"Yeah, well, if I'd known you were going to drop a backpack on my head, I'd have brought a football helmet."

I started to laugh, and Sue joined in before raising a hand to her head. "Ouch. That hurts."

I pulled my hat from my head and held it out to her. "Here. Put this on."

"Thanks," she said, carefully pulling the hat over her head. "This is quite a sacrifice for you, giving up your hat. I mean the way you think a hat is an absolute necessity up here. Lord knows you made that point firm enough when you were trying to convince me to bring one."

"Actually, it's not much of a sacrifice at all," I answered. "I have an extra hat in my backpack."

"You brought *two* hats? *You* who were so insistent that we pack only what we absolutely need?"

"Things happen to hats up here, Babes. They get soaked in the rain or fall into the water or get blown off in windstorms or . . ."

"Okay," she interrupted. "I get it."

"So what are you two going to do now?" asked the scoutmaster, returning to us. "Stay here tonight?"

"I'm not staying here," Sue replied. "I didn't like this place when we first arrived, and I certainly don't like it now." She looked up at me. "I'm not staying here."

"We're not staying here," I agreed.

"Well, then," the scoutmaster said to Sue, "the boys and I'll carry your pack for you." I waited for the argument, the protestation that she could carry her own pack. But when it didn't come, I realized how exhausted she was.

"Maybe we *should* stay here tonight," I suggested.

"No way," she replied, reaching for my hand. "Help me up, and let's get started."

* * *

As we approached the scouts, one of the older boys stepped forward. "We found these under the bear cache," he said, extending his hand to Sue. Dangling from his fingers were her glasses, the lens remarkably intact but the frames twisted into an almost comic caricature of their former shape.

Sue worked to reshape the glasses as the rest of us slipped into our packs. When we were ready, she put them on and, tugging my hat down over her ears, asked, "How do I look?"

The glasses sat at an angle on her face. One lens jutted above her left eyebrow, and the other dipped below her right eye. She smiled and batted her eyes flirtatiously.

"You look wonderful," I responded. "A little like Harpo Marx with a hangover, but wonderful."

She grinned and, reaching up, tried to straighten the glasses. "And you, my dear," she said, stepping into line behind the departing scouts, "have such a beautiful way with words."

*   *   *

I extended my hand to the scoutmaster as we stood on the bank of Isaac Lake. "I owe you more than I can say."

"No, you don't," he replied. "You'd have done the same for me if one of my boys had been hurt."

"And I still owe you a Scotch," I reminded him.

"I haven't forgotten. If you catch up to us somewhere, I'll take you up on that."

Below us the scouts had just finished tying the last of their equipment into their canoes. While Sue and I had opted for staying in this first campground on the lake, the scoutmaster had chosen to take advantage of the afternoon light and gain a few more miles.

Isaac is the largest and deepest lake on the circuit, twenty-four miles long and liberally sprinkled with campgrounds. It's also the lake with the most numerous and most aggressive bears. Here at the shallow end we would have less chance of a bear visit. When I explained this to Sue, she readily agreed to make camp early.

"Besides," Sue said, looking around, "I like this campground. It's open, it has a nice view, and we're the only ones here once the scouts leave. I'd love to have a camp entirely to ourselves."

We stood together, watching the scouts paddle out into the lake. "Hey," I called to the scoutmaster as his canoe turned left in front of us, "I don't know your name."

"Nathan," he answered.

"I'm Bob."

"I know. And your wife is Babes."

"Only to me," I corrected him. "To the rest of the world, she's Sue."

"Oh, . . . sorry," he replied. "Well, she's a brave lady." He cupped his hands around his mouth as his canoe floated down the lake and yelled to Sue, "You're a brave lady."

"Thank you," Sue called in return. She leaned into me, playfully. "I'm a brave lady," she said in a lower voice.

"Yes, you are," I answered. "Now why don't you find a nice place to rest, and I'll start setting up camp."

"I'm a brave lady," she answered, frowning, "but I'm not a *lazy* lady. I'll help with camp. But," she added, "when you put the packs into the bear cache tonight . . ."

"Yes?"

She pointed across the campground into the trees. "I'll be way over there."

*   *   *

That night after dinner, Sue and I sat on the lake shore, watching Nature put on a show for us. Shafts of orange, red, and purple colored the sky and undercoated a few lacy clouds in the sunset.

"You know," I said, sipping my coffee, "if this were a painting, no one would believe it. 'Not real,' they'd say. 'No sunset has that many colors.'"

"It's so beautiful," Sue replied. "Thank you for bringing me here."

"You can say that after today?"

"I can say that after today."

"You know what?" I said. "I think we should stay here tomorrow instead of going on down the lake."

"Really?"

"Sure. Why not? We've agreed not to rush the first half of the trip. Why not just hang out here for a day? What's that old saying about red sky at night being a sailor's delight? Looks like a good day tomorrow. We could sleep in late, have a leisurely breakfast, fish, play around in the canoe . . . whatever. What do you think?"

"Sleep in?" Sue answered dreamily. "Sounds good to me."

We sat a few more minutes in silence, watching the colors blend and fade. Then Sue leaned into me. "Would you really have done it?" she asked.

"Done what?"

"Sacrificed your Scotch for me?"

"Babes," I replied, kissing her on the undamaged side of her face, "I would sacrifice Grand Marnier for you."

"Ooh," she responded, looking up. "You're such a romantic."

Loading a bear cache

Sue modeling her new look

DAY 3

A LAZY MORNING

I awoke to the sound of voices and canoes dropped carelessly on the ground. After listening for a couple of minutes, I turned my head toward Sue. She was lying on her side, facing me, one eye open, the other squeezed shut.

"The Germans are here," I whispered.

"I know. They certainly mistreat their canoes."

"Definitely rentals," I answered.

After their voices had faded into the woods as they started the return portion of their portage, I stuck my head out of the tent, checked the weather, and then ducked back inside. "It's beautiful," I reported. "Warm sun and blue skies. We should have a great day."

"What time is it?" Sue asked, yawning.

I glanced at my watch. "Almost nine-thirty. Ready for a pancake breakfast?"

"You bet," Sue said, struggling to free herself from the sleeping bag. "I'm starved."

*　　*　　*

A chorus of *guten Tags* and *guten Morgens* greeted us as the Germans returned to drop their packs by their canoes. In an amazingly short time, they had tied in their gear and paddled off down the lake.

"Auf wiedersehen," Sue and I waved. The campground was silent once more.

"They *are* a happy group," Sue laughed as she put some water on our pack stove to heat for the dishes. "*Noisy* but happy."

She straightened up. "Why don't you see if you can catch some fish while I clean up around here?"

"You sure?" I asked. "How's the head?"

"Oh, I'd almost forgotten about my head. You'd better get going before I start feeling sorry for myself and change my mind."

*   *   *

"Any luck?" she called an hour later as I nosed the canoe into shore.

"Nope, the fish just weren't cooperating. But see that island straight across from us?" I asked, pointing over my shoulder with my paddle. "On the other side is a really nice beach. Why don't we pack a lunch, grab our books, and do a little sunbathing? It's a great spot."

Sue was already sorting through the food pack for appropriate picnic items before I reached her.

*   *   *

SKINNY-DIPPING WITH MINK

"This," I said, lazily stretching as we lay side by side on the beach, "is the life."

"This," Sue answered, looking over from her book, "is very nice. Very nice, indeed."

I stood up, stepped over our shoes and socks, and moved to the water's edge. "I'm going swimming," I announced. "This shallow water should be a little warmer than the rest of the lake."

I was already stripped to the waist. I hop-stepped out of my pants and stood looking at the water. Then I impulsively dropped my shorts and walked into the lake.

"What on God's green Earth are you doing!" Sue yelled.

"I'm going German," I grinned.

"Shame on you. What if somebody comes by?"

"All the travel's on the other side of the lake. They can't see us from there. Want to join me?"

"Are you suggesting I skinny-dip with you?"

"The water's great," I lied. "You don't know what you're missing."

"Honestly . . . skinny-dipping. I suppose you did that all the time in Estacada."

"Actually, this is my first time."

"Really. I'm surprised."

"Oh, we're quite civilized in Estacada," I answered. "We always wear swimsuits. And whenever we dress up to go somewhere, we wear shoes and everything.

"So how about you?" I continued. "Ever skinny-dip?"

"No," Sue shook her head. "The Portland public pools had rules against it."

"Tempted, though, aren't you?" I prodded.

Sue moved to the edge of the water and began unbuttoning her shirt. "I don't dare get my head wet," she said. "I'll have to keep my hat on."

"*My* hat," I corrected her.

"Your hat," she agreed. "Besides, if I keep the hat on, you won't be able to brag that you talked me into going completely naked in the light of day."

"That's true. Also, everyone knows a partially dressed woman is more alluring than a completely nude one. The hat'll be a sexy touch."

And it was.

*　　*　　*

We sat on our kneeling pads, our backs against the sun-warmed side of the overturned canoe. "This feels so good," Sue sighed, digging her toes into the sand. "If I didn't have to do it in front of other people, I think I could become a nudist."

"*I'm* other people."

"You don't count."

"Thanks a lot."

"You know what I mean. Now how about we change the subject?"

"Sure. Maybe we could talk about what's been moving around on that weed bank over there," I answered, nodding toward a large patch of high, wavy grass.

"Where? I don't see anything."

"Right there," I pointed. "See there it goes again."

As if on cue, a quick movement parted the grass, and a small triangular head popped up. A black head with tiny cupped ears, beady eyes, twitching nose.

"Shh," I breathed. "Don't move."

The head disappeared, the grass rustled, and a long, ropy body suddenly bounded from the weeds onto the open sand. With the peculiar hunching movements of the weasel family, the animal advanced a few feet and then stopped, leaned forward, and studied us, black eyes staring, whiskers moving as it sniffed the air.

Without turning my head, I whispered, "That's a mink."

"It's so cute," Sue answered.

As if alarmed by the sound of our voices, the mink suddenly sprinted to the left in a furry blur, slid to a halt, reversed itself and darted back to its starting position. It stood still, tensed as if ready to blast off again in its demonstration of speed and agility.

"What's it doing?" Sue asked.

"I don't know. He looks as if he's challenging us to a fight. Or maybe a foot race. In either case, we'd probably lose."

"How do you know it's a he? Could just as well be . . . Wait. There's another one." A smaller chocolate form had suddenly leaped from the grass. It shouldered up to the bigger black one. Both stared at us for a moment, and then they sprang into a darting, erratic dance of stops and starts over the sand.

"They're playing," Sue laughed. "Look at them."

"They certainly seem to have decided we're no threat."

"Do you think they're mates? Is this some kind of boy-girl thing?"

"Could be," I said, watching the bigger mink chase the other across the sand. "Hopefully, that's it."

"Why *hopefully?*"

"Because pound for pound they're pretty vicious animals. If this isn't play, that small one could be in serious trouble."

"No way. They're not fighting."

At that moment the mink reversed direction. "Look," Sue continued. "Now the little one's chasing the big one."

"Definitely a girl-boy thing," I grinned.

"Wait a minute," Sue said, turning to me, her face clouded over. "Didn't you use to kill these?"

"Babes," I sighed, "in three years of trapping, I caught only two mink, and those were by accident in my muskrat sets. Wherever you find muskrats, you'll find mink because muskrats are their favorite prey. But I never intentionally tried to trap mink. They were always way too smart for me."

"Oh, you just trapped poor little muskrats then."

"Well, the muskrats paid for my gas. I made most of my money trapping beaver."

In front of us, the mink had stopped their display and stood still, watching us, as if dismayed by our conversation about trapping.

"Could you do it now?"

"Trap? No, I couldn't do it now. Look. I was a teenage boy. Running a trap line was a macho thing. And the money was good."

"Well, I'm glad you couldn't do it now," Sue smiled.

The mink had disappeared into the grass once more, but an occasional rustle now and then suggested their game of tag continued.

Sue leaned over and pulled our day pack from under the canoe. She rummaged through it and then stood up and aimed our camera at me.

"Don't you dare," I said, jumping up.

"Smile," Sue grinned.

"Don't," I warned.

"Smile."

Reaching down, I grabbed the kneeling pad and dropped it into a strategic position just before the shutter clicked.

"I can't believe you did that," I said, shaking my head. "Sometimes you're just a little too playful."

"And sometimes you're such a fuddy-duddy," Sue replied, advancing the film. "This'll be a great picture to share with our grandchildren some day."

"That'll be a picture we don't share with anyone."

At that moment, over Sue's giggling, we heard the distinctive clunk of a paddle striking a canoe gunnel. "Someone's coming," Sue gasped, reaching frantically for her clothes.

Having instinctively ducked behind the canoe, I peered over it. "Relax," I said. "They're clear over on the other side of the lake. That's just the way sound carries on water."

A string of five canoes moved past our campground. "Must be the Seattle group," I guessed. "Good. Let them get a day ahead of us. We won't have to scramble for campsites."

"Our mink are deserting us," Sue said, looking back toward our sandy beach. The tiny heads cut vees in the water as they swam toward the opposite shore.

"Well, we'd better think about leaving, too," I answered, reaching for my pants. "The shadows are beginning to lengthen. It'll start cooling down soon."

"Okay. But I hate to leave. This seems like our own special island."

"Well, I think the mink have prior claim, but they didn't seem to mind sharing."

"They were so cute," Sue responded, buttoning her shirt. "They might be my favorite animals so far. Let's see," she began, ticking off a count on her fingers. "We've had a nutty loon, a couple of moose, some frisky mink. And this is just our third day. I wonder what'll pop up next.

"I can't make specific promises," I answered, turning over the canoe, "but I'm sure we'll see something every day. You can pretty much bank on that up here."

"I hope so," Sue replied, fastening the day pack to the middle thwart. "Seeing all these animals in their natural environment beats the heck out of a visit to the Portland Zoo."

We moved the canoe into the water, and I held it as she positioned herself on the front seat. I thought about what she had just said. She was still the Portland girl with all points of reference inside the city limits.

"Yes," I said, "this is much better than a visit to the Portland Zoo."

What we couldn't know at the time, of course, was that Sue's next sandy-beach wildlife encounter would involve an animal much larger and much more frightening than the mink we were leaving behind.

A quiet evening paddle

My favorite time of day

DAY 4

LEAVING OUR ISLAND BEHIND

"**I hate to leave,**" Sue sighed, looking across the lake toward our island. "Yesterday was the best day so far."

"Well," I replied, straightening up from the canoe, where I had just finished tying in the last pack, "you really don't have much to compare it to."

"Meaning?"

"Meaning the first day we were forced to portage an extra three miles because of the crowds and then we had to spend the night in a cold camp, kept awake by a drunk German chorus. And the second day I dropped a pack on your head, cut off your hair, and contemplated sewing you up with a dull needle and some industrial-strength thread."

"Aw . . . , but the third day," Sue smiled, "I skinny-dipped for the first time in my life and sun-dried while being entertained by a couple of supercharged mink. And all that on my own private beach."

"Look up," I replied, pointing. "Not a cloud in the sky. And it's only nine o'clock in the morning. With luck this weather will hold, and we'll get in a good day's paddling. Above all, we have to take advantage of water like this." I nodded toward the lake's surface. Hardly a ripple distorted the reflection of the blue sky overhead and the green timbered ridge across the lake.

"I know," Sue agreed, moving toward the canoe. "It's just that yesterday was so perfect. I don't see how we can top that."

"Perfect is nice, Babes, but perfect is a bonus up here. Remember we need to be ready to handle the bad as well as the good."

"Oh, *really?*" Sue answered, sweeping my hat off her head and dropping her chin so that I was looking at the latticed butterfly bandages climbing the bald swath I had scissored through her hair.

"Touche," I grinned sheepishly. "Point taken."

BEARS AND PIT TOILETS

The weather did hold. I was shirtless by the time we put in on a sand spit for lunch, my sweat-soaked T-shirt draped over the pack in front of me. We had paddled for three hours, reaching the dogleg where Isaac Lake turns from east to south. Ahead stretched nineteen miles of paddling before we reached the place where this wide, deep lake emptied abruptly into a rushing torrent of water called "the chute." I had said little about the chute to Sue, figuring we still had a couple of days before she had to worry about that particular adventure.

A quick lunch, twenty minutes of rest stretched out on the sand, and we were on our way again.

*　　*　　*

By two o'clock, Sue was noticeably tiring. She was shifting from kneeling to sitting more and more frequently, a sure sign of paddling fatigue. So when we reached the next campground, I suggested we call it a day. She was quick to agree.

The campground was empty, but as we walked through it, Sue became increasingly nervous. "I don't like this place," she finally admitted. "It has a bad feel."

"Why? It seems all right to me."

"I don't know," she replied, shaking her head. "It just doesn't feel right."

"Well," I said turning back toward the lake, "the last time you had that feeling about a campground, something really bad *did* happen, so let's move on. Okay?"

"Okay," Sue nodded, visibly relieved.

*   *   *

"Anything with red on it," Larry said, holding up the spinner. "Stan and I have come up here four years in a row, and everything we've caught has been on something with red on it."

Sue and I had paddled only twenty minutes after having left what she was now calling the "spooky campground" when we saw two men by a canoe beached under an overhanging bank beside the mouth of a stream. The heavyset man was sitting on a log, eating a sandwich. The second, small and wiry, was battling a fish, his rod bending and jumping in his hands.

"I have to put in and see what he's using," I said to Sue, turning the canoe toward the bank.

Larry and Stan were talkers, the kind who relish a new audience. Stan was a school administrator in Abbotsford, and Larry, who lived in nearby Chilliwack, was in construction. Every summer they left their wives for a boys' vacation, fishing and camping in the province.

I glanced at the twelve-inch trout on the log, where Larry had placed it after throwing the guts into the lake. "Some people say not to do that," Larry remarked, kneeling to rinse his knife, "but it's either that or carry the innards with you until the next fire. Bury it and the bears'll dig it up. Once they do that in a place, they keep comin' back. Bears are kinda like people, I guess. Figure out where the free handouts are and then hang around looking for more."

"Speaking of bears," Stan interjected, "did you see those along the bank between the last campground and here?"

"Bears?" Sue asked. "What bears?"

"You didn't see 'em, huh? We were going to eat lunch in that campground, but we had just put in when a sow stepped out of the brush and came right toward us. She had a couple of cubs in tow. It wasn't a good situation, so we hightailed it outta there."

"Yeah, but we still had trouble shaking her," Larry added. "She tracked us for about ten minutes or so, those little fellows strugglin' to keep up. She'd walk along the bank and ever so often go off into the woods. Just when we thought we'd lost her, she'd come out on the bank and walk along with us again. But finally she disappeared."

"Thought you might have seen her," Stan concluded.

"You say she kept up with you for ten minutes or so?" I asked.

"Right."

"But it took us only twenty minutes to paddle down here from that campground. That means she was ten minutes away from here and heading this way when you last saw her. And how long ago *was* that? Thirty, forty-five minutes ago?"

"What'd you say you taught down there in Oregon?" Larry asked. "English, was it? You sound more like a math teacher to me.

"Anyway," he continued, picking up the trout, "it *might* be time to take this fellow and get along down the lake. Nice to meet you two. Looking forward to bumping into you again."

Sue and I watched the pair of them load day packs and fishing gear into their canoe and push out into the lake. As they were pulling away, I looked at Sue, who looked at me. Without a word, we began walking rapidly toward our own canoe.

Only when we were safely out on the water, did Sue speak. "That campground where they saw the bears was the spooky campground, wasn't it?"

"Babes, if I ever doubted your instincts—and I'm not admitting I ever have—I will never doubt them again. Now, let's put some distance between ourselves and this place. We need to find a campground for the night."

"One without bears, I hope," Sue offered. "That story made me more than a little uneasy."

"Well, I warned you this is the worst lake for bears, but that was just one incident. A little scary, but just one incident. We can't let it get into our heads, or we won't enjoy one of the nicest lakes on the circuit."

"I'm not even going to ask you to qualify *nicest*," Sue replied, returning her paddle to the water, "but I do want you to know I think it's a relative term at best. And I fail to see how the worst lake for bears can be one of the nicest lakes on the circuit."

"You're right," I answered. "Everything is relative. Now, are we going to have a philosophical discussion of relativity, or can we just get on down the lake and find a nice—and I use the word in its *nicest* sense—a nice campground, where we can set up camp and then sit quietly on the bank while I wrap my right arm around you and my left hand around a Scotch?"

"*That*, my sweet," responded Sue, "is the *nicest* thing you've said all day."

*   *   *

"This is Betty Wendle campground," I said, as we drifted toward a collection of canoes—some overturned and others upright, skid marks in the mud showing they had been dragged rather than carried from the water's edge.

"They're a little like the Germans, aren't they?" Sue observed.

"What do you mean?"

"Not very careful with their canoes."

"That's not all they're not careful with," I responded. "Look over there." Scattered on a log were several large lake trout. A short distance away, a couple of packs leaning against a tree were ringed with various food items: a loaf of bread, a large mustard jar with a table knife jammed into it, a collection of dirty dishes attracting a cloud of flies that equaled those circling the fish.

"Let's not even bother stopping," Sue said. "We definitely aren't going to consider staying with them."

"Too late," I replied. One of the campers was walking down the slope to the water's edge, coffee cup in one hand, his other motioning us toward an opening between the scattered canoes.

"But we're not staying," Sue demanded.

"Right. We'll stretch our legs, be sociable for a few minutes, and then be on our way."

*   *   *

"Can you believe those people?" Sue asked twenty minutes later as we left the campground behind. "Garbage everywhere. That young boy tossing chunks of a peanut butter sandwich to the chipmunks. Yuk! You'd think people from Seattle would be smarter than that."

"Well, I don't know why you'd think that," I answered, "being a hard-core Portlander and all. But you're right. They aren't showing much common sense. And I'd be willing to bet they'll have trouble before the night's through."

"Oh, really?" Sue sniffed. "Peanut butter on the grass, dirty dishes lying around, and those fish crawling with flies. What's up with that, anyway? Do they think fish have to decompose before they're ready to cook? They're trout, not Beijing duck. Anyway, even a novice like me can see they might as well hang up a sign: 'Bears, looking for a good time? Check *us* out.'"

"That's not the half of it," I replied. "That campground they're in? Betty Wendle? It's one of the worst campgrounds for bears on the whole circuit."

"What! And you were thinking about staying there tonight!"

"Well, I thought you were tired."

"Listen, fella. You don't bed me down with bears just because you think I'm tired. *Tired?* I can't believe you. We're outta here." And with that, she leaned forward and began setting a pace that belied any suggestion she was tired.

Wow, I thought to myself. *She's becoming a really strong paddler.*

* * *

"I need a bathroom," Sue threw over her shoulder fifteen minutes later.

"There's a campground just around that next point," I answered. "We'll stop there, but we're not putting in for the night. It's too close to Betty Wendle, and I want to put some distance between that Seattle group and us. I think they're trouble, and I don't want to be stuck in a campground with them somewhere down the way."

As we rounded the point, we saw that the campground was empty.

"It's tempting," I said, as we pulled the canoe from the water, "but I'd just feel better if we could distance ourselves from the Seattle bunch a little more."

"Can we talk about this later?" Sue asked, hurrying up the trail to the pit toilets on a rise above the camp.

* * *

"I want to stay here," Sue announced upon returning.

"Why?"

"I like it. It's a clean campground."

"Really?" I answered, looking around. "It's a nice enough campground, but cleaner than other campgrounds? I don't see it."

"Well, you haven't seen the toilets."

"Why? Is there a little man up there handing out towels and expecting a tip?"

"For your information, the park rangers have been here cleaning out the toilets."

"Huh?"

"Yeah, the park people have been cleaning them out."

"You mean sweeping them?"

"No, I mean really cleaning them out. The toilets have big holes dug beside them where the rangers have tunneled under to remove the . . . the . . . Well, you know what."

I studied her for a moment as she stood there, arms folded across her chest, proud of her discovery. Then I said, "Show me."

*   *   *

Sue was right. Huge holes gaped alongside each toilet. I walked along the edge of one, knelt for a closer look, and then stood up. Taking Sue's arm, I turned away and, pulling her into step beside me, started down the trail to the campground. "We're not staying here."

"What? Why not?"

"I'll explain later. Let's go."

*   *   *

"Okay," Sue said as we approached the canoe. "It's later. So explain. Why can't we stay here?"

"Babes, I know you haven't had much experience with pit toilets, but they aren't cleaned out and reused. They are basically toilets over holes in the ground. When the holes reach—what do I call it? Saturation point? When the holes reach this point, the toilets are removed, and the holes covered with dirt. New holes for the toilets are dug somewhere else. You don't clean out a pit toilet."

"Then who dug those holes?"

"Who do you think?"

"I don't know who did!" Sue exclaimed, exasperated. "I was happy thinking the park rangers dug them. Now you want me to nominate someone whose purpose in burrowing under outdoor toilets isn't to clean them? Get real."

"Bears, Babes. Bears dug them."

Her eyes widen. "Why?"

"Because people are lazy. They don't want to carry out their garbage. They don't want to bother burning it. So they dump it in the toilets. Along with fish guts and anything else they want to get rid of. They think no animal would be attracted to the camp if it meant going into a toilet. But that's a major difference between humans and animals. Animals aren't nearly as finicky when it comes to free meals.

"And I want you to consider this," I added as I moved the canoe into position to shove off. "Bears *are* like humans in one respect. They don't work any harder than circumstances demand. A bear digs a hole only as big as he needs."

"And those," Sue finished for me, "were really big holes."

"Really big holes," I agreed.

She stepped into the canoe and made her way to the bow. Kneeling on her pads, she picked up her paddle and turned to look back at me. "Well, what are you waiting for? The sooner we make camp somewhere, the sooner you can have your Scotch."

"Now you're talking my language," I said, shoving the canoe off the soft sand and stepping over the gunnel. "And I might add, it's a much more pleasant subject than pit toilets."

"And *I* might add, my dear," Sue responded, "if you ever tell this story to anyone, I guarantee you'll regret it for the rest of your life."

"Now would I do that?" I asked, J-stroking the canoe into position to start down the lake.

"I'm *serious*," Sue replied as we fell into our rhythm. "This is just the kind of story you love. Big-city girl meets the real world."

"Okay, I won't tell anyone about the pit toilets."

"Promise?"

"Promise."

"Wait a minute," Sue said, lifting her paddle and turning to face me. "Did you have your fingers crossed when you said that?"

"Now how could I have my fingers crossed and paddle at the same time?"

Sue studied me as I assumed my most hurt, innocent look. Finally, as she turned back to the front to resume paddling, she said, "Okay, I guess you couldn't."

But I could. And I did.

AN EVENING WITH THE SWISS

The lakeside trees were casting long shadows when we reached the next campground. Like the last, this campground was empty. "It's close to five o'clock," I noted, looking at my watch as we glided into the takeout beach. "We really need to get settled for the night." When Sue didn't bother to respond, I knew how exhausted she was.

The campground was a little unusual in that it had two levels, campsites near the water and a newer section on a plateau farther up a trail, tent sites and fire pits pushing back against a slope of Douglas firs.

"I like this spot," Sue noted, dragging a foot across a tent site as she kicked away small rocks and twigs. "In fact, I like this campground. It has a nice feel."

"Okay," I replied. "Then this is it. And having the entire camp to ourselves suits me just . . ."

"What's that!" Sue yelped as a high whistle cut through the quiet of the trees.

Before I could answer, the sound repeated. Then it came again and again in quick, high blasts.

"Is that a police whistle?" Sue asked.

I shook my head. "If you were in Portland, that'd be a police whistle. Here it's a bear whistle."

"Bear whistle? The bears have whistles?" Sue grinned.

"No," I answered, playing into her game. "People have bear whistles."

"And why do people have bear whistles?" she asked. "Do bears come when you whistle? And, even more important, do you want them to?"

Before I could answer, she added, "That noise is really becoming annoying. I wish it would stop."

"Me, too," I replied. "But for a different reason than mere annoyance."

"And what does that mean?"

"You remember the first day when I told you that on the trails we should carry on conversations in normal to louder-than-normal volume?"

"Sure. I remember almost everything you tell me."

"Okay. Why?"

"Because," she responded in a clipped voice as if she were a recorded message on an answering machine, "bears . . . do . . . not . . . like . . . to . . . be . . . sur . . . prised."

"That's right."

"So what you're finally getting around to tell me is that bear whistles are used by people to avoid surprising bears."

"In most cases," I answered.

"In *most* cases," Sue repeated. "Once again, what does *that* mean?"

"Well," I shrugged over the incessant screeching of the whistle below, "the only recourse people on the circuit have when threatened by bears is to make noise. You know, like beat tin pans, yell, or . . ."

"Or blow whistles," Sue finished my sentence for me.

"Right."

"So let me see if I get this straight. You think someone on the beach is trying to scare off a bear?"

"Yes," I answered. "Maybe," I qualified when I saw the look on her face. "Anyway, I think we should get down there. Our packs are still in the canoe." I turned toward the trail leading to the water's edge.

"Hold it," Sue commanded. "If they *do* scare off a bear, doesn't it head up here in our direction? And isn't it royally ticked off?"

"*Our* direction is down there," I answered, over my shoulder. "We need to protect our packs."

I had taken several steps toward the beach when I realized Sue wasn't following.

"Come on," I commanded, turning to face her. "If a bear is trying to get into our food supply, we need to be there."

"To do *what*? Wrestle the bear for our food while that idiot with the whistle referees? No thanks," Sue said, shaking her head. "I'm staying right here."

I looked around at the darkening forest. "Okay," I said, turning back to the trail, "suit yourself."

I had walked maybe five yards before she called out, "Wait a minute. I'm not staying here alone. Wait up. I'm coming."

I took her hand to help her down a cut bank. "I thought you might," I grinned.

"Shut up," she growled, punching me in the upper arm. "*You* don't know me."

"Oh, I *know* you," I answered as we turned to make our way toward the shrill whistle that had not let up since the moment we first heard it.

The whistle cut through the air again and again as we walked into the lower section of the campground. There we found a young woman, clothed in a red-and-black checkered jacket; baggy European-styled hiking pants, cinched below the knees with leather laces; and black wool stockings above heavy high-topped hiking boots. Clinched tightly in her teeth was the source of our annoyance, a nylon strap trailing from it to a loop around her neck.

"Oh, hello," she gasped, a little out of breath from her last blast.

Before we could respond, a voice from the lakeside called out, "Christina, please quit blowing that whistle. By now every bear in the park knows we're here."

Sue leaned toward me. "I don't know who that is, but I like him."

As if in answer, a dark-haired young man, dressed exactly like the whistle-blower, climbed into the campground from the beach below. "You have to excuse Christina," he grinned as he approached us. "She has an ungodly fear of bears."

"Oh, as if you *don't*," the young woman protested.

"Well, I have to admit I do," he answered. Stepping over a muddy spot in the trail, he offered an introduction as he approached. "My name is Albin. This woman with the amazing ability to blow a whistle is my wife Christina."

There was a European timbre in his voice, but I couldn't quite place it. German, but not quite German. It escaped me.

"We're Bob and Sue," I replied.

"And where are you from," Albin responded, shaking my hand.

"We're from Oregon."

"Oh. Ore-e-gone."

"No, Ore-e-gun," I corrected.

"This is good," Albin laughed. "My chance to hear the difference between American English and Canadian English."

"And you?" I asked. "I can't quite place your accent."

"We're Swiss. But we've been in Canada for a little over a year now. We're becoming very much New-World people."

"Okay," I answered, nodding. "I heard German, but I thought I heard something else as well."

"Very likely," Albin laughed. "We Swiss speak German, French, and Italian, depending on where you are in the country. And some of us just mix them all up and see what comes out."

"Well, you should add English to your list," Sue offered. "You speak our language very well."

"Oh, yes, of course. English is taught from a very early age in our schools. If I might say," he continued with a sly grin, "we Swiss probably speak better English than many of you Americans do."

"That's a topic we'll have to discuss over coffee tonight," I offered, delighted with this young couple. "That is, if you're staying here."

"What do you think, Christina?" Albin turned to his wife.

"You didn't see any signs of bears in the camp?" Christina asked, directing her question to Sue.

Sue patted the young woman's arm in a motherly gesture. "Believe me. I wouldn't be here if I had."

Visibly relieved, perhaps as much by the maternal comfort as for the absence of bears, Christina turned to her husband and nodded.

*　　*　　*

Albin and Christina set up camp in a site two over from ours, and I was impressed with how precisely efficient they were. It was a clean, orderly camp, a picture-perfect replica of our own.

After separate dinners in the two camps, the young couple joined Sue and me for the coffee I had offered earlier. Albin was mysteriously vague about his employment with the Canadian government, which had recruited him to work for their military establishment. "I'm an engineer," was all Albin would offer about his job. "I'm here on a two-year contract to work on various projects."

"Albin is too modest," Christina said, beaming at her husband. "He was selected for this position from dozens of applicants."

"Well, the point is," Albin interjected, obviously a little embarrassed by his wife's gushing admiration, "we have only two years in this country, and we plan to see as much of it as we can. You know what we did last summer? We spent two weeks canoeing on the Yukon River."

"Excuse me," I replied. "I'm a little puzzled. I really envy your canoe trip on the Yukon. But for people who have spent that kind of time in grizzly country, you seem to have a . . . a . . . I don't quite know how to say this . . . a *heightened* awareness of the black bears down here. Somehow, I would think people who had dealt with grizzlies wouldn't be so concerned about black bears."

"That's all right," Albin replied. "You can say it. You Americans have a perfect idiom for what Christina and I feel. We're scared spitless of bears. And it's precisely *because* we spent two weeks in grizzly country that we have such respect for them. As for grizzlies versus black bears, if I may paraphrase one of your American poets, 'A bear is a bear is a bear.' But that fear is not going to stop us from enjoying this magnificent country."

"Tell them about today," Christina coaxed.

Albin sipped from his coffee cup before responding. "We put in at a campground midmorning for a break, and a mother bear came out of the brush straight for us. We had to back out of there, or she would have climbed right into the canoe, I'm sure."

"How do you know it was a mother bear?" Sue asked.

"Because," Christina picked up the thread of the story, "just after she came out on the beach, two of the cutest babies walked out behind her. They were darling."

"A sow and two cubs," I interposed. "Sounds like the same bear two Canadians told us about today.

After I had related Stan and Larry's story, I concluded, "I suspect the park rangers are going to have to do something about that bear before she causes real trouble."

"Like what?" Christina asked. "They wouldn't kill a mother with two babies, would they?"

No one had an answer to that question. I thought to myself, *Who's at fault here? The people who come into this beautiful country, upsetting the delicate balance of nature, or the animals who instinctively view these travelers and their goodies as a daily buffet table?*

"So are you getting an early start tomorrow?" Albin asked, changing the subject, something I had begun to recognize as a useful skill in his relationship with his wife.

"I think we will," I replied. "I figure if we do, we'll make the end of the lake by midday. Then we can move on down to McLeary for tomorrow's camp."

"Really? So you're going to run the chute and the roller coaster tomorrow?"

"I plan to," I answered, avoiding eye contact with Sue.

"Mind if we paddle with you? We'd like to be off this lake by tomorrow night ourselves. I understand the bear problem diminishes on the other side of the circuit."

"Sure," I said, venturing a glance at a glaring Sue. "That'd be good."

*   *   *

Sue waited until we were in our sleeping bags before asking the questions I had been dreading since Albin and Christina said good night and left for their camp site.

"So what's the chute? And what's the roller coaster?"

"Oh, haven't I mentioned them?" I asked in the most innocent tone I could assume.

"No. To best of my recollection—and I believe I would remember such a thing—you have not mentioned a chute or a roller coaster."

"Well, it's kind of funny, really. A quirk of nature, kind of. You see, the end of this lake empties somewhat abruptly into a river. Needless to say, the volume of water is high, and the exit is an exciting adventure for people in a canoe. That's the chute."

"And the roller coaster?"

"Well . . . ," I hesitated, seeking the right words, "the river is rather rambunctious for a stretch."

"Rambunctious," Sue repeated. "And you simply forgot to mention this?"

"I was going to tell you when the time came," I replied, lamely.

After a long silence, Sue said, "But tomorrow we'll be off this lake and rounding the corner to the other side of the circuit?"

"If everything goes right, I think we will."

"And the other side doesn't have the bear problems this side has?"

"Not even close," I comforted.

"Good," she sighed. "I'm tired of bear stories spoiling our trip. Thank God, they've all been secondhand. I just want to get off this lake without coming face to face with a bear."

"That's my plan, Babes. I plan to leave Isaac Lake behind without a single bear encounter."

"That's your plan?" she whispered. And in a few minutes, I felt her relax into my shoulder, breathing deeply as she slipped into sleep.

That was my plan. However, what did Robert Burns say about the best-laid plans of mice and men?

DAY 5

PADDLES, COOKING GEAR, AND QUASIMOTO

I woke early to a cool-gray sky. Night-spun spider webs glistened with dew in the predawn light. From the bear cache, I brought down our day pack with its toilet articles, small cooking pot, one-burner stove, and coffee. With this pack slung over my shoulder, I made my way to the lakeside for some much-needed solitude.

A steaming cup in my hand, I looked across the lake at the far-side forested slope. Dark, shadowy, silent. The lake itself, glassy and still. Except for a small splash around the bend to my left—probably a trout feeding on surface-struggling insects—I heard nothing. No rustling of small animals in the underbrush, no wing-whipped flights overhead. Nothing. Quiet is so underrated in our world today. I needed this early morning stillness, this transcendental moment in such a magnificent setting.

In the cool air, I sipped my coffee as I watched the sky kaleidoscopically transform from shadowy gray to purple, to red, to orange, to light-diffusing blue as the sun rose over the ridge behind me. On the lake, mist hovering over cold water dissipated into warming air. Sparkles of sunlight lit the surface. Night had given way to day.

*   *   *

When I returned to camp, I found Albin and Christina packing their gear, moving quietly, obviously concerned about waking their neighbors.

"Oh, hello," Albin waved. "We thought you were sleeping in."

I lifted our tent flap to check on Sue. All I could see of the scrunched figure in her sleeping bag was the back of a tousled head. Dropping the flap, I lifted my finger to my lips in the universal "shh" signal and stepped toward Albin and Christina, who had made their way into our campsite.

"Sue was really exhausted yesterday," I began in a low voice. "She's still sound asleep. I'm not going to wake her until she's ready."

"Well," Albin began, glancing at Christina, "I know we planned to paddle together today, but if you're going to get a late start, we think we'll leave as soon as we can."

"No problem. The water's perfect. You should take advantage of these conditions while they last."

Both smiled with relief. Obviously, they had worried about upsetting us with the decision not to wait for late-arising Americans.

"But we'll wait for you at the chute if you want," Albin offered.

"Unless you can see us coming down the lake when you get there, just go for it. Chances are if we don't get away for another hour or so, we won't run the chute until tomorrow.

"And that's okay, too," I added. "People do the first half of the circuit much too fast. They rush through to the other side, only to find they wish they'd spend more time here. The other side is fun, but this side has a grandeur that you lose once you turn the corner."

"I've heard that," Albin, said.

"Can I ask you something?" he continued.

"Sure. What?"

"Well, I've been impressed with your camp. Christina and I have stayed in campgrounds with some other people who, quite frankly, scared us with their careless ways."

"Oh," I grinned. "Spent some time with the Seattle people, did you?"

Albin nodded. "Them and some others. Anyway, I wanted to ask you about some things you do I've never seen before."

"Like what?"

"Well, for starters, why do you hang your paddles from tree branches?"

"Porcupines."

"Porcupines?"

"Yeah. They like salt. They'll gnaw on your paddle handles."

Albin looked puzzled, and then a light went on. "Oh," he said, lifting one finger like a college professor making a point. "Right. Perspiration."

"Uh huh. The sweat from your hands works into the handles. And eventually the paddles can become a porcupine's midnight snack."

"Good," Albin said. "I learned something new. Now, why do you put your cookware in the bear cache? I'd be very surprised if you didn't use non-scented soap, so once you've washed everything, why do you put it in the trees?"

"That's a good question," I answered, "but it involves a bear story. Are you up to that, Christina?"

She nodded but reached instinctively for the bear whistle on the cord around her neck.

"My third trip I was camped at Betty Wendle," I began. "I had never put my pots and pans in the cache before that night, thinking, as you do, that animals wouldn't be interested in clean, scentless metal.

"Early in the morning I awoke to the sound of something messing with the pots. I figured a squirrel was poking around, so I unzipped the tent and stuck my head out."

"And?" Christina breathed.

"There by the fire pit was the biggest bear I've ever seen. It had been pawing my pots and pans and was now standing on its hind legs holding my plastic two-gallon water jug in its front paws. While I watched, it took a bite out of the jug. When it realized the contents were only water, it threw the jug down in obvious disgust."

"What'd you do then?" Christina asked, wide-eyed.

"I started yelling at it. I told it to get the . . . well, to leave the premises."

"And did it?" Albin asked.

"Uh huh. Dropped down on all fours and waddled off into the brush."

"You scared it away just by yelling at it?" Christina asked.

"Oh, I don't think it was scared. Probably just annoyed. And I couldn't really tell if it had left the campground or just circled around to snoop in an area with less noise."

"So what'd you do?" Christina continued.

"I zipped up the tent and got back into my sleeping bag."

"You went back to bed?" Christina gasped. "How could you do that?"

"Well, what were my options? I figured it was too big to get into the tent with me, and I wasn't big enough to go out there with it."

"Good thinking," Albin agreed.

"Anyway, since that time, I've put the cookware in the cache at night."

"I want you to know I heard all that," came a voice from inside the tent.

The flap pulled aside, and Sue's head emerged. "Good morning," she beamed.

I heard a gasp and turned to Christina, who had instinctively stepped back, her hand to her mouth.

Oh oh, I thought, looking back at Sue. She had forgotten to put on my hat. In the shaved half-moon on her head, now sprouting a three-day stubble, the butterfly bandages pulled at the puckered wound.

Sue's smile faded, and she looked to me for an explanation. I raised a finger to my head and tapped it.

"Oh," Sue responded, her hand coming to her own head. I couldn't tell if she was instinctively covering the wound or slapping herself alongside the head for having forgotten the hat.

She ducked back into the tent and reappeared with the hat pulled firmly down to her ears. "Is that better?" she grinned.

"What happened to your head?" Christina asked.

"Oh, that? No big deal. Bob just dropped a pack on me."

"What!" Albin and Christina answered in unison.

"Yes," Sue grinned, nodding. "He dropped a pack on my head."

"How?" Albin questioned.

"It's a long story," I interrupted, "and I wouldn't want to hold you two up from your early start."

"You poor thing," Christina cooed, kneeling in front of the tent.

"It's all right," Sue smiled. Then she leaned farther out and stage-whispered in a wife-to-wife conspiratorial tone, "Think how much mileage I'm going to get out of this."

*   *   *

"They're a nice couple," Sue said as we stood on the beach, watching Albin and Christina paddle down the lake. "But shame on you, scaring that young girl with another bear story."

"*Me* scaring her?" I returned as we began walking back into the campground. "What about *you* with your 'Quasimoto Meets the Wolf Man' routine?"

"Quasi who?"

"Quasimoto. You know, the hunchback of Notre Dame."

"Oh, *that* Quasimoto."

"Yes, that Quasimoto. How many Quasimotos do you know?"

"I like that name," Sue answered, holding back a branch for me. "I think I'd like my first grandson to be named Quasimoto."

"Oh, that'd be great," I agreed. "It'd make him tough and all. You know, like Johnny Cash's 'A Boy Named Sue.'"

"*Hey*, nothing wrong with the name Sue."

"A good name for you," I agreed. "But for a boy? Not so much. And Quasimoto? Not so much."

"We could call him Quasi," Sue continued as we entered our campsite. "Or," she brightened, "Moto."

"Oh, good idea," I answered. "Better yet, why not twins? One Quasi and the other . . ."

Moto!" Sue leaned into me. "I love it. Perfect. That'll be it then. Quasi and Moto."

"Won't their parents have something to say about all this?"

"No more than you did," Sue smiled, "when you thought you could rag me about scaring Christina, and I turned the conversation to a debate about my grandsons' names."

Man, I thought to myself. *When am I going to realize, once and for all, who's really in charge here?*

*   *   *

Conditions were perfect as Sue and I pushed off from the beach. As our canoe knifed through the clear blue-green water of Isaac Lake, I couldn't imagine a place I'd rather be.

"I figure it's about six miles to the end of the lake," I had told Sue as we loaded the canoe. "With these conditions, our final day on Isaac will be a nice leisurely paddle with an early arrival at our last camp on this side of the circuit."

And with that innocent prediction setting the mood, we embarked on what would prove to be the most danger-filled day of our trip.

SUE AND THE BEAR

Two hours later, we beached on a long sandbar, the sky laced with light clouds and the water slightly ruffled by a soft breeze that had come up in the last few minutes. The inviting sun-warmed sand coaxed us into extending our lunch break.

"Babes, I'm going to try a little fishing up there," I said, pointing to the north end of the sandbar, where a small stream emptied into the lake.

"Sure," she smiled. "I'll rinse out our cookware and pack everything back into the canoe."

Ten minutes later, I had just cast my spinner and was working it through the wide ripples at the mouth of the stream when I felt a tap on my shoulder.

I had never seen Sue's eyes as wide as they were at that moment.

"What is it?"

"*Bear,*" she whispered.

"Bear?"

"*Bear.*"

"Where?"

"*There,*" she thumbed over her shoulder toward the canoe.

"Okay," I replied, reeling in my line. "Let's go."

Approaching the canoe, I saw no sign of a bear. "Where is it?"

"It was right there," Sue answered, pointing to the cleared space where we had eaten our lunch, a mere fifteen feet from the canoe.

At that moment from the corner of my eye, I caught a movement in the low brush at the edge of the sandbar. I froze and then turned my head slowly. There, peering at us through the brush, was a teddy-bear head."

"Oh," I laughed. "It's just a baby."

"That's not the one," Sue replied.

"Right," I answered. "Come on. Let's get our gear into the canoe. Don't worry about tying anything down. We're outta here."

We paddled into the lake, and then I turned the canoe parallel to the sand bar. At the site of our lunch break, a large female and a cub scratched and nosed through the sand.

As we watched them, Sue explained what had happened. "I was rinsing our bowls when I heard something moving in the sand behind me. I thought you had come back, and I asked why you had quit fishing so soon. When you didn't answer, I turned around, and there it was. Right there behind me.

"What was really scary was the way it was standing up on its hind feet, waving its front paws and sniffing the air, swinging its head side to side."

"What'd you do?"

"I stood up slowly and began backing up the beach. When it didn't seem all that interested in me, I went to get you."

"Perfect, Babes," I replied. "You did everything just right."

"I *did,* didn't I?" Sue smiled. "Who says I'm just a city girl?"

"Who, indeed?" I answered.

We watched the bears as they searched for any tidbits we had left behind. Finally, the mother sat down in the sand exactly where we had sat and looked out at us as if to say, *Couldn't you have spared* something, *you tightwads?*

SURFING IN A WINDSTORM

On a body of water as big as Isaac Lake, prudent canoeists stay near the shore. But a large lake is seldom symmetrical. The shoreline recedes into bays and extends into promontories. Following that kind of shoreline can add hours to a day's paddling.

Usually I wouldn't succumb to the lure of the easy way. But in leaving the two bears behind, we had paddled farther from shore than we normally would. Also, in the next hour, the warm sun and hypnotic rhythm of steady paddling had lulled me into carelessness. I had allowed us to drift into the middle of the lake.

I was brought out of my daydreaming by a blast of wind that ripped through us from behind and flattened Sue's shirt against her back. At the same moment, the temperature dropped as a black cloud pushed over us. I looked to the shoreline, where the tops of trees were swaying in the wind.

"Babes," I called, "we have to get into shore." But when I started to turn the canoe, a wave smashed into the bow and pushed us back into our original course. Then the worst nightmare of canoeists hit us. Whitecaps. A moment before, we had been idling down a sun-filled lake. Now we were being slammed with cresting waves. Turning broadside to the waves would swamp us.

"We can't turn," I shouted. "We have to outrun it. Paddle, Babes! Reach and pull! Reach and pull!"

We had to keep the canoe moving faster than the waves. Allowing the water to dictate the speed and direction of the canoe invited disaster. In our circumstances, we had no control over the direction, but we *could* control our speed—*if* we stayed ahead of the current.

As I worked with deep strokes, fighting to keep us from slipping off the waves into a broadside position, I could feel the bow swinging from side to side.

"Babes," I yelled over the wind, "you have to paddle. You have to paddle, Babes!"

"I'm trying," she fired back over her shoulder, "but I can't reach the water!"

"What!"

"I can't reach the water!"

I looked to her paddle. Sue was right. She couldn't reach the water. We were atop the crest of a huge wave, and Sue, out front of the wave, was paddling thin air. As if our canoe were a surfboard, we rode the wave down the lake. Then it swept through us, and we slammed down into the water once more.

Again and again, the waves tried to twist us to one side or the other, to force us into a position that would swamp us. My shoulders on fire from J-stroking us back on line, I marveled at the fight Sue was putting up in the bow. Together, we battled a lake that had turned from gentle giant into raging monster.

Suddenly Sue called, "I see it! Up ahead. The end of the lake. And there's the campground! Right straight ahead of us!"

Looking past her shoulder, I could see it, too. Waves crashed into the bank above the area where I expected to see the takeout beach. But there was no beach. It had disappeared under the waves. Overturned canoes were scattered on the upper bank, where they had been rescued from the beach. A large crowd of people watched our frantic approach.

If we stayed on the same course, the waves would smash us headlong into the bank. Frantically, I searched the shoreline for an alternative landing site.

To our left, a huge tangle of drift logs and branches jutted from the water. From the vantage point at the height of a wave, I saw what appeared to be a protected lagoon behind the logs. If we could find a way through that snarl of logs and branches . . .

The bow rose on the next wave, and I was looking at the treetops in the campground. Then it smashed down again, and I could see an opening in the tangle of logs. We might just fit if we came straight in.

"Babes," I yelled, "I'm going for that opening in the drift logs. When I say, 'Now,' quit paddling, grab hold, and don't let go."

Sue waved her paddle to let me know she had heard and then leaned into her stroke once more. Another giant wave lifted the canoe and slammed it down in perfect alignment with the gap in the drift logs.

"*Now!*" I shouted.

I pulled for the opening. Just as we started in, Sue yelled, "Look out!" At that moment, I saw it, too. A submerged log across the opening, just a foot or so below the surface of the water.

The aluminum canoe shuddered and screeched as we tore over the top of the log, plowed through the water behind the tangled driftwood and ground to a perfect stop on a gravel beach.

I stared at the paddle in my white-knuckled hands. Then I heard it over the wind. I needed a moment to register the sound.

Applause.

I looked up to see the crowd of canoeists on the bank above us. They were giving us a standing ovation.

BEAR RAIDS AND FRENCH CUISINE

The storm passed over us almost as quickly as it had arrived. The winds let up, the waves diminished, and the takeout beach reappeared.

Albin and Christina, who had been in the crowd watching us come in, helped carry our gear to one of the last open campsites.

"This is one of the biggest campgrounds I've seen so far," Albin said, "but it's already filling up because of all the people blown off the lake. And I would guess now that the wind has died, more people will follow."

As if in answer to his comment, Sue pulled at my sleeve. "Look," she said, pointing up the lake. A flotilla of canoes had appeared, people who had taken refuge during the storm and were now making their way to the campground.

"It's gonna be so crowded tonight," I groused.

"It *is,* isn't it?" Sue answered, her eyes sparkling.

As the canoes arrived, we began recognizing familiar faces. "There come the Seattle people," Sue announced. "And look. I think that's Larry and Stan." A few minutes later, she pointed to four canoes. "Oh, look! The Boy Scouts!"

"Those four people are from Williams Lake," Christina chimed in, pointing to a pair of beautiful wooden canoes cutting through the water. "We camped with them a couple of days ago. They're really nice. You'll like them." I glanced at Albin, who gave me a knowing grin. Obviously, Sue and Christina were kindred spirits.

*   *   *

Two hours later, Albin and I checked the damage inflicted upon my canoe when Sue and I had plowed over the log blocking our entrance to the gravel beach. A large ragged knot had ripped a long crease in the hull.

"Aluminum is the only way to go," Albin commented as he ran his hand along the crease. "Fiberglass or wood probably would have shattered."

"That's true," I agreed, "but I still hate any dings to this canoe. It's my baby."

"*Ding?*" Albin asked, glancing up from his kneeling position. "What is *ding?*"

"Ding," I answered. "It means a dent or scratch on something."

"Oh, well then, this is more than a ding. But look at it this way. A canoe is like the human body. Over time it accumulates scars, and each scar has a story. This scar is a beauty because it has such an *exciting* story behind it."

"You're right. Dangerous experiences do become dramatic adventures in the retelling. Take Sue and her bear, for example," I added, remembering Sue's excitement an hour earlier when she had described her encounter to Albin and Christina.

"And speaking of Sue," Albin answered, looking past my shoulder, "here come the ladies back from their scouting trip."

Sue and Christina had been like a couple of cooped-up cocker spaniels as they gave the late arrivals time to set up their camps. "Come on," Sue had finally said, unable to wait any longer. "Let's see how everyone handled the storm."

As they approached us, Sue called out, "There are thirty-five people in camp, and almost everyone had bear troubles today, but only two stories are better than mine.

"You were right about the Seattle people at Betty Wendle," she continued, lowering her voice. "They had bears in the campground all night. They said they didn't get any sleep at all.

"Anyway, are you two ever going to stop playing with the canoe and come back to camp? You're missing all the fun."

*   *   *

As Sue and I parted from Christina and Albin to return to our separate campsites, she continued to rhapsodize over her conversations with the newcomers. "Nathan checked my head and . . ."

"Whoa. Wait a minute. Nathan?"

"Yes, Nathan. That's the scoutmaster. Remember? Anyway, he checked my head and said you and he should go to medical school, it's healing so well. Made me feel a little funny, though. We must have looked like a couple of grooming chimps, him running his hands through my hair that way."

"Oh, and Christina was right about the Williams Lake people. They're really fun. They invited the four of us over for coffee tonight. Of course, we said we'd bring our own.

"And speaking of food supplies," she ran on, "two different groups had bears actually take their food packs away from them."

"Those would be the two stories that top yours?"

"Yes, but *I* faced off on a standing-up bear all on my own, so I think my story is right up there with the best. Maybe not the best, but right up there with the best."

"Also, you get novice points," I added. "Those other people were probably wilderness-hardened veterans. Until this trip, the only large hairy creatures you had ever encountered were in the mall at Christmas. Today, all by yourself on a lonely sand spit, you took on a . . . what did you call it? A standing-up bear? I haven't heard those other stories yet, but I think with novice points, you're in the running for first place."

"Aw," she grinned, "you're just saying that because you love me."

"Well, that, too," I agreed.

*   *   *

"We knew it was bear trouble even before we put in," Larry said, leaning forward from his sitting position on the log by our fire pit. "They were hollering at the top of their voices. Their stuff was scattered all around their canoe."

Larry and Stan had strolled into our campsite shortly after Sue and I returned from the beach and were describing a rescue they had pulled off earlier in the day.

"We went into the campground, following the noise, and there they were, up in the bear cache. A young couple, hanging on for dear life." He paused for dramatic effect and then continued. "At the foot of the ladder, one of the biggest bears I've seen up here was pawing at their packs. He'd bat one and then the other, pull them back and bat them again.

"We tried to drive him away. Yelled. Threw rocks. Nothing fazed him. Finally, he settled on which one was the food pack and dragged it away into the woods. And that was that. It was gone. The pack. The food. The sleeping bag still on the pack's frame. Everything. Gone."

"Didn't you look for it later?" I asked. "He probably just dragged it out of sight and ripped it open. You might have been able to salvage something."

"Nah," Stan shook his head. "We'd have heard that. He was just flat-out gone."

"Besides," Larry added, "when we finally coaxed that French couple down, all they wanted to do was get out of there."

"French?" I asked. "Like in Canadian French?"

"Nope," Larry grinned. "Like in *French* French. They don't speak much English. Not that we took any time to chat, anyway. They just threw their remaining pack into their canoe and cut out. Stan and I didn't catch up with them until their adrenalin petered out. But since arriving here, they've been the center of attention. Someone told me they're from Paris."

"Anyway, it's a good thing we didn't hang around looking for their food pack," Stan said. "The bear had that campground staked out, and he would have been back."

"How do you know?" Sue asked.

"Because another group here had the same trouble in the same place. They had just started to unload their canoes when that big bruiser came out of the brush and headed straight for them. But there were *four* of them, and they didn't climb into the bear cache like the young French couple. They stood their ground. Well, maybe not right at the canoe, but they did the right thing instead of running. They yelled, beat some tin cups, got him to go off."

"But not before he'd ripped open one of their packs, scattered everything, and made off with a couple of snacks," added Larry. "At least they didn't lose all their food like this other couple."

"What are the French couple going to do now?" Sue asked. "Bob says we'll probably take five more days to complete the circuit."

"If they really push it from here and the weather holds," Larry answered, "they could be out of here in three, three and a half days."

"Without food?"

"Oh, they'll have enough food. Everyone in camp is giving them something. They're kind of celebrities right now. Got a plastic trash bag half full of food already."

"Really!" Sue replied and looked over at me. I knew what was coming.

"We should give them something," she said. "What can we give them?"

"Our rations are figured pretty close to what we need. I suppose we could give them a couple of our lunches. If worse comes to worse, we can skip lunch."

"We've already used up our bread," Sue pointed out. "What do we have left for lunches?"

"Top Ramen."

"Top Ramen? That's it? These people might starve, and all you'd offer them is Top Ramen?"

"It's nutritious. It's filling. If, as you say, they are in danger of starving, they should be *happy* with Top Ramen."

"They're French."

"So?"

"I don't think the French eat Top Ramen."

"Well, I'm sorry, but I forget to pack the escargot."

"Oh, it'll probably be all right," Sue conceded. "They'll be thankful for anything we can give them, I'm sure."

Ten minutes later, Sue and I, armed with three packets of Top Ramen, set out on a culinary adventure in which we would come face to face with the French version of gratitude.

*   *   *

The French couple looked like a pair right out of Hollywood. She was tall, thin, and blonde. He, with his five-day growth, was handsome and virile. A small crowd surrounded them, offering them food items, which they accepted as if these gifts were their entitlements, their rightful bounty from the little people.

When our turn came, I took a packet of Top Ramen from Sue's hand and held it out to the blonde.

She studied the packet, mystified. Finally she said, "Noooodles? Zis nooooodles?"

"Oui."

"Oui? Parlez vous Francais?"

"Non. Parlez vous Anglais?"

"Non . . . Oui . . . Leetle," she said, holding up her hand, first finger and thumb an inch apart.

"Well, you don't have to parlez vous Anglais to cook this stuff. It has pictures. See?" I held up the packet and pointed. "Water. Pot. Boiling. You know, bubbling." Here I waved my hands up my chest as if I were immersed in a hot tub. "Add noodles and spices. Wait three minutes," I continued, holding up three fingers. Voila! Soup's on."

She studied the pictures and then, turning to her companion, said something that made him laugh. I didn't literally understand a word of what she had said, but in body language and facial expression, I understood exactly what she had said. *"Do you believe these people? They need pictures to cook."*

She turned back to me. "Merci." Holding the packet by one corner as if she were lifting a dead rat by the tail, she dropped the Top Ramen into her food-collection bag. Tugging my sleeve, Sue pulled me away.

"Can you believe that broad?" I muttered as we walked through the campground.

"I told you I didn't think they'd want Top Ramen," Sue whispered. "Doesn't it make you wonder, though?"

"Wonder what?"

"Well, they didn't seem familiar with freeze-dried food. If they weren't carrying freeze-dried, what kind of food *were* they carrying?"

"They're French. They probably had some nice kidney cutlets, a juicy batch of tripe, maybe even a supply of baby eels. Of course, they'd accompany all that with a heavy, overpowering white sauce to disguise the fact they were eating such disgusting stuff."

"Quit it," Sue grinned, poking my arm. "You're making me feel sorry for the bear that took their food."

"What really frosts me," I grumbled, "is that we gave them three of our lunches, and they probably aren't going to eat them, anyway."

"One," Sue corrected.

"One?"

Pulling two packets of Top Ramen from under her sweatshirt, Sue asked, "Do you really think I'd let that blonde stick her nose up at our offer and still get all three?"

"You never cease to amaze me," I grinned.

"I know," she smiled.

I put my arm around her shoulder. "You're feeling pretty good right now, aren't you?"

"I guess. Why?"

"Oh, I don't know. I'm just under the impression you're in a really good frame of mind."

She thought a moment. "Yes, I think I am."

"Great. Because you know what? I think it's time we check out the chute."

"The chute? Really? Can we see it from here?"

"Sure. It's right over there," I answered, pointing to the south side of the campground.

"What about the roller coaster? Can we see that, too?"

"Uh huh. Well, we can see *some* of it from there, anyway."

"Okay," Sue said. "Let's go see what kind of trouble you're going to get me into tomorrow."

LOOKING AHEAD

The transition from Isaac Lake to Isaac River is abrupt. A lake twenty-four miles long suddenly funnels into two miles of river fraught with rapids and impassible cascades.

The park headquarters provides each party of canoeists a map and a written commentary on the circuit. The description of this trip down Isaac River includes warnings such as "Chute and upper part of river navigable for experienced canoeists only" . . . "riotous waters" . . . "mildly thrilling" . . . "log jam" . . . "foaming cascades unnavigable" . . . "river plunges thirty-five feet over a ledge" . . .

Sue had never seen this written description. I hadn't exactly hidden the commentary. I had simply not mentioned it. As we stood on a high bank looking down at the chute and the beginning of the roller coaster, a roiling torrent of water cascading out of sight around a bend, I set out to replace her very sensible apprehension with an anticipation of the adventure in running this river.

"We run the chute, whip down the roller coaster—which is great fun—and end up in a quiet, deep pool behind a massive log jam. There we take out and portage around a stretch of water that is a little too challenging for canoes. Then we put in and paddle about a mile until we reach a takeout on the other side of the river. It's important we take out there because the river goes over a waterfall a little farther on."

Sue, not taking her eyes off the river, said quietly, "Yes, I can see the merit of taking the canoe out at that point."

"Yeah, well, from there we portage down a rather steep trail to a pretty little lake called McLeary. It's quiet and green, nestled in sweet-smelling cedars. It feels good after the rush of the river."

"And we camp there for the night?"

"Oh, no, we'll be there around lunchtime if we get an early start."

"So where do we go then?"

"McLeary is tiny. We'll cross it in ten minutes or so. Then we enter the Cariboo River."

"More river paddling?" Sue asked, her voice beginning to rise.

"Oh, it's nothing like *this* river. Yeah, it twists and turns a little, and it has some swift rapids, but *nothing* like this river."

"Well, that's good, I guess."

"Uh huh." I replied, encouraged. "It just has one little problem."

"And *that* is?"

"Uh . . . well . . . it's a glacial river, so it's always milky with silt. That makes it hard to see sweepers, and there are quite a few of them in the river."

"Sweepers?"

"Yeah. Trees in the water. It's something we really have to watch out for. But a good thing is the river is pretty shallow. I saw a young couple swamp there on one of my trips, and when they stood up, they were only waist deep in the water."

"So that's the one good thing?" Sue replied. "If we swamp, we might be able to stand up in the river?"

"Actually, we'd be a lot better off than they were. You know how careful I am about tying in everything when we paddle. Well, they weren't. I waded out and helped them, but we could salvage only their big packs. They lost a day pack, a couple of cameras, fishing gear, jackets, even a pair of boots."

"But if *we* swamp, we won't lose our gear," Sue responded.

"Nope. Stuff might get wet, but we won't lose anything."

"I don't suppose it has occurred to you that I'm some of the stuff that'll get wet. I'll be standing in water coming from a glacier somewhere. Probably be a little cold, don't you think?"

"It won't happen," I assured her, "because we'll have the best eyes in the world looking out for the sweepers."

"Whose? Yours?"

"Nope. Yours. You're in the bow, so your job is to look out for sweepers, overhanging tree branches, rocks, all that stuff. See how much faith I have in you? When we run the Cariboo River, you'll have the most important job in the canoe."

"Where do we end up?"

"The river empties into Lanezi Lake. It's big. Almost ten miles long. That's where we'll camp if all goes well."

"A big lake sounds good. After those rivers, being on a big lake again will probably be nice."

"I suppose."

"What do you mean, you suppose? What aren't you telling me about this lake."

"No big thing, really. It's just that of all the lakes on the circuit, Lanezi is the only one that hates me."

"What!"

"It hates me. But," I quickly added, "it couldn't possibly hate *you*. I think you'll be my good-luck charm, and Lanezi will welcome us with open arms."

"Okay," Sue said after a stretch of silence while I tried to gauge her response. "Let's see if I have this right. We come through that gap." She pointed to the chute, where Isaac Lake was pouring into Isaac River. "Then we fight our way over those rapids," she continued, pointing to the roller coaster. "Next we walk around a section of water even worse that these, a stretch so bad no canoes go there. We get back in the river and paddle to a place, where we have to be sure to get out again, or we go over a waterfall. We carry the canoe and our packs down a steep trail to a little lake, where we put in again. Then we go down a milky river full of trees waiting to dump us. And by the way, where the responsibility for avoiding that is entirely mine. And finally we come out on a big lake that hates you."

"That pretty much sums it up, all right."

"Well, I'm glad we had this little talk. I feel much better now. But I do have one more question."

"What's that?" I asked, taking her hand as we began our return to the campground.

"Is it too late to go back the way we came?"

THE BEAST AND THE SCORPION

That evening after dinner, Sue and I, carrying cups of coffee, made our way to the campsite of the Williams Lake people. Christina and Albin were already there, and Stan and Larry joined us a short time later.

As we sat around the fire, talking and laughing, I glanced at Sue. She was as happy as I had seen her the entire trip. Good company, a warm fire, entertaining stories—these were the components of Sue's world.

Christina and Sue had been right about the Williams Lake people. They *were* fun. A pair of neighboring couples who spent their vacations together, they were typical British Columbians: hearty, down-to-earth, fun-loving people. This was their third canoe trip together, but even though they lived so close to the Bowron Lake circuit, they had never visited the park.

"It seems strange, doesn't it?" commented Frank, the elder of the two men. "I guess when you have something in your backyard that attracts people from all over the world, you think 'I can do that anytime' and off you go to play in *their* backyards. But now that we're finally doing it, we'll probably be like Stan and Larry here and come back year after year."

The conversation turned inevitably to bears. The Williams Lake people had heard only a secondhand version of Sue's story and prompted her to tell it. I watched her eyes sparkle as she recounted the incident, already fine-tuning it, and I knew this narrative would become a favorite in her repertoire of stories for those future grandchildren, Quasi and Moto.

After Larry and Stan had laughed their way through another description of the French couple clinging to the trees above a bear pawing through their packs, I turned to Albin and Christina, who had been quiet to this point.

"What about you two?" I asked. "You were chased off a beach yesterday, weren't you?"

"Yes," Albin replied, "but it was a basic cut-and-run incident. Nothing like these two stories."

"Maybe," I pressed. "But you told me you have a special respect for bears because you canoed theYukon River last year. I'll bet you have some good stories from there."

"Again," he shrugged, "cut-and-run stories. Our encounters were mostly with grizzlies, and they're much bigger than black bears and have a bad reputation, so they're even a little scarier, I suppose. But we were never as close to them as Sue was to that bear today."

"Cut-and-run stories?" Larry interrupted. "You didn't really run from a grizzly, did you?"

"No, I was just trying to employ an American idiom. Did I use it wrong?"

"Well, I don't know about that, but I do know grizzlies like nothing better than to see something try to run from them. Makes them think whatever's running is good to eat, and grizzlies love to chase down food."

"Yes, I know. We didn't run from any grizzlies. We just backed out of a number of situations that could have turned bad."

I didn't like the way this exchange was going. Larry seemed to consider this young Swiss a novice, probably because of Albin and Christina's being so uptight about bears. I knew, however, that anyone who had canoed the Yukon *was* experienced. Larry's lecturing Albin on grizzly behavior seemed presumptuous.

"We have them here, too, you know," Larry continued. You don't see them very often, but occasionally you do. Stan and I have seen them on the Bowron River."

"The Bowron River?" Sue asked. "Is that another river we'll be on?"

I nodded. "But as Larry said, we probably won't see any grizzlies. They stay pretty much to themselves."

"Mostly they're there when the salmon are running," Larry explained. "Leave them alone, and they'll leave you alone."

"You told me we'd be out of bear country when we left this half of the circuit," Sue said, her voice rising.

"No, I didn't. I said bears weren't as much trouble on the second half."

"Grizzly bears aren't as much trouble? Are you kidding me?"

Putting her hand on husband's arm, Christina artfully changed the course of the conversation. "Albin, you *do* have a great story. Tell them about the scorpion."

"Scorpion?" I asked. "You ran into a scorpion on the Yukon River?"

"No," Albin laughed. "We were in the Sahara Desert. But that's not something you want to hear about."

"Are you kidding?" I answered, looking at Albin through an updraft of red sparks as Frank stirred up the fire. "That sounds like a *great* story."

"Come on, Albin," Christina encouraged, pulling on her husband's sleeve.

"Okay," Albin sighed. "When Christina and I were married, we honeymooned in North Africa." I could feel his audience settle into comfortable listening positions. From man's beginning, no form of storytelling has had a more powerful hold than the well-turned oral narrative. And one that begins " . . . we honeymooned in North Africa" couldn't hold more promise.

"Our plan was to rent a Land Rover in Morocco and drive into the Sahara for three or four weeks. But rentals for that long were expensive. Then we ran across a touring group that was selling off its vehicles, and we bought *The Beast* for little more than we would have spent for a rental."

"*The Beast?*" Larry asked. I was pleased to see he was already caught up in the story.

"Uh huh. That's what we named him. *The Beast*. He's a Land Rover with all kinds of grillwork welded on his top and sides. Bob and I were talking today about how scars on people and canoes have stories behind them. Well, if that holds true for cars and trucks, *The Beast* is a rambling encyclopedia of narratives. Unfortunately, most of those stories occurred before we bought him, so Christina and I have had to make up much of his history."

"We tell people he's a reject from the Foreign Legion," Christina added.

"So you still have him?" Sue asked, unconsciously falling into their description of the Land Rover as a living, breathing being.

"We do," Albin smiled. "After our trip we took him back to Switzerland, but he was never happy there. All those narrow, winding village roads, you know. However, when we decided to come to Canada, we thought what better place to take *The Beast*? And we were right. This country is perfect for him."

"In fact," Christina added, "we have always smiled about friends who miss their pets when they travel, but for the past four days, we've worried about *The Beast* all alone back there in the parking lot."

"Forget *The Beast*!" Larry interrupted. "What about the scorpion?"

"Oh, right," Albin grinned. "A couple of days into the desert, we came over a dune, and *Bam*! We hit something, and *The Beast* ground to a stop as if we had thrown out an anchor. I had the tires deflated by about half the normal pressure to make driving in soft sand easier, but that also lowers the vehicle closer to the ground. We had obviously snagged on a rock or something.

"I could hardly see under *The Beast* because of the depth of the sand. But after I dug out a little, I saw a broken spring hanging down, digging into the ground."

"Here's where I come in," Christina picked up the narrative. "I got out the jack, a sand mat, and the tool box and took them to Albin."

"A sand mat?" Stan asked.

"It's a metal grid that people carry to help them get out when they bury their rigs in the sand," Albin answered. "I wanted it to use it as a foundation for the jack.

"I got *The Beast* high enough to crawl under with a length of heavy wire and a pair of wire cutters, intending to tie up the spring so we could move again."

Albin paused a moment. "Just after I had stretched out under *The Beast* and reached up to push the spring into place, the jack slipped, pinning my arm between the axle and the spring. I couldn't move."

"I jumped in and tried to straighten the jack to lift *The Beast*," Christina began, "but all of a sudden I heard Albin say in a low, clear voice, 'Don't do anything. Don't move anything. Remain perfectly still.'"

Albin picked up the story. "I was looking at a scorpion, about three inches long, on my pinned forearm. It was acting nervous, its tail arched over its body, lightly tap-dancing on my skin."

"That was bad," Stan breathed.

"Very bad," Albin agreed. "There are over thirty different varieties of scorpions in the Sahara, and at least four of them are lethal to humans."

"So what did you do?" one of the Williams Lake people asked.

"I waited. It kept dipping its head forward as if it were tasting my skin. I had sweat running down my arm, and I thought it was drinking. Later, though, I read that Sahara scorpions don't drink liquid in the normal way. They absorb all the moisture they need from the bodies of their prey."

"And then?" Stan pressed when Albin hesitated.

"It began to move. It crawled down my arm, up my shoulder, and out of my sightline. I could feel it moving around my neck. Then I couldn't feel anything. My arm had gone numb, and I thought my shoulder and neck had, too. I was sure it was still there, somewhere near my aorta."

"But it wasn't?" Sue asked, hopefully.

"I guess not because finally I moved my other arm and nothing happened."

"Then what?" Sue asked, leaning forward.

"Then *I* came to the rescue," Christina beamed. "I got the jack straightened up and managed to lift *The Beast* off Albin."

"And the scorpion?" Sue pressed.

"Nowhere to be seen," Albin answered. "Sahara scorpions bury themselves under the sand or under rocks to escape the hot sun during the day. I figure we hit a rock that not only broke *The Beast's* spring but also woke my little friend from his nap. After he had checked me out, he must have gone off to find a more peaceful spot."

We all sat for a moment, waiting for someone to say something. Finally, Larry broke the silence. "*That* is a great story, my young Swiss friend. You may not have been as close to a bear as Sue here, but a cold-blooded scorpion crawling around on your neck while you're pinned down? Now *that* is a great story!"

Albin stood up, grinning. "Thanks. Now I think it's time Christina and I turn in. We have a big day tomorrow."

"Don't we all?" I agreed, rising and taking Sue by the hand to pull her to a standing position.

"So you're planning to run the chute tomorrow?" Stan asked.

"Sure. Aren't you?" I replied.

"Maybe," he answered. "But I think we're in for a storm."

He looked up through the trees. The rest of us instinctively followed his glance. The stars were gone. Heavy black clouds obscured everything. And as if in answer to our uplifted faces, raindrops began tapping the fir boughs overhead. Over the crackle of the fire, we could hear the wind picking up as the storm moved down the lake.

*   *   *

I woke in the night to the drumming of heavy rain on our tent fly and the eerie groaning complaint fir trees make when swaying in the wind. Turning from my side to my back, I propped my head in my hands and listened to the symphony of rain, wind, and moving trees.

In the darkness beside me, Sue whispered, "You awake?"

"Uh huh."

"What does this mean for tomorrow? Will we still go if it's stormy like this?"

"Well, tomorrow's mostly portaging and running rivers, so it wouldn't be like today when we were caught out on the lake. Still, I don't like hiking through the woods in a high wind."

"How come?"

"Widow makers."

"Widow makers?"

"Uh huh. Dead branches that break off in the wind and come down like a shot, sometimes like a javelin pitched right at you. When I worked in the woods with my dad, widow makers were a logger's worst fear. Sometimes you don't even hear them, but even if you do, you don't know which way to run without looking up. And looking up at that moment is something you really don't want to do."

"So what if it hits me instead of you?"

"Huh?"

"I was just wondering," Sue giggled. "Would that make it a *widower* maker instead of a widow maker?"

She scooted closer and draped her arm over me, nestling into my shoulder. "So we don't go if it's windy. But what if the wind quits and it's still raining? Do we go then?"

"Unless our visibility is restricted on the rivers, there really isn't any reason not to go ahead in the rain. But paddling in rain isn't much fun. And we didn't come up here just to push forward without having fun."

"You mean fun like today when I was frantically trying to reach the water on that high wave, and you were yelling at me to pull or else? You mean like that kind of fun?"

"Admit it," I answered. "You *did* have fun. You may not have realized it at the time, but danger can be fun if you come through it with flying colors the way you did today. At least, fun in hindsight."

"Well, I'd just as soon not have any more fun like that on the rest of this trip, thank you very much."

After a few minutes of silence, Sue said, "So as I understand it, if it's windy, we don't go because the storm gods will hurl widow makers at us. If it's raining, we don't go because you don't think that would be fun. Do I have it right?"

"Right."

"If it's raining, I get to sleep in?"

"As much as I'd like to get ahead of this crowd, if it's raining, you get to sleep in."

I felt her relax against me. Though my arm was going to sleep under her head, I lay still, waiting for the moment she drifted off before trying to slip the arm out from under her. But when Sue felt the movement, she shifted her weight, setting my arm free.

"Still awake?" I whispered.

"Yes," Sue replied, snuggling back into place beside me. "Now don't interrupt. I'm busy praying for rain."

DAY 6

THE CHUTE AND THE
ROLLER COASTER

Sue's prayers were not answered. Though the next morning was gray with heavy clouds and soggy from the night's storm, the wind had let up, and the rain had stopped.

After a quick breakfast of oatmeal and coffee, we broke camp, packed our gear, and started off down the portage trail that follows the banks of Isaac River.

"Tell me again why we're doing this?" Sue asked.

"Carrying our backpacks instead of putting them in the canoe for this part of the trip?"

"Exactly. Why carry them when we could cut our time in half by paddling with them?"

"It wouldn't cut our time in half," I answered, a little exasperated because I thought I had explained this well enough back at camp. "The chute and roller coaster are really fast as far as time goes. We get to the takeout place at the cascades before you know it. So loading everything into the canoe and tying it down and then fifteen or twenty minutes later having to untie everything and unload it to portage it around the cascades takes more time than it's worth. This way, we just carry the packs to the final put-in spot on the river. Believe me. This is better. Besides," I continued, "a light canoe is much easier to handle in fast water than one loaded down with gear."

"That all sounds good, but none of it is the real reason you don't want the packs in the canoe," Sue challenged.

I turned to face her. "What do you mean?"

"There's a real chance we can swamp in this stretch, and you don't want our gear in the canoe if we do," she replied. "*That's* what I mean."

"Well, there's that, too," I grinned. "But my other points are valid as well."

"Okay. Just don't sugarcoat things. All right? I'm a big girl now. I took on a bear. I took on the worst storm this country could throw at me. I can handle this river. Okay?"

"Okay," I agreed, turning back to the trail. *Man,* I thought to myself as we set off again. *City girl become Davy Crockett overnight.*

*   *   *

We were almost back to the campground when we had to step aside for a young couple setting off down the trail, he in the lead with their canoe over his shoulders and she with a day pack on her back, a camp stove in one hand and an ax in the other. A couple of muted morning greetings passed between us as Sue and I stepped aside to let them by. I didn't recognize them from the campground the day before and wondered aloud if they had already paddled this morning from another campground up the lake.

"I don't know," Sue responded. "But my question is why are they carrying their canoe down the trail? Aren't they going to run the chute and the roller coaster?"

"Evidently not. Quite a few people don't. Guess they take the Park Service's brochure seriously."

"Why? What does it say?"

"Says this stretch of the river is for experienced canoeists only."

"*I'm* not an experienced canoeist," Sue objected. "Why aren't *we* portaging our canoe past this stretch?"

"You *are* an experienced canoeist. You earned your stripes yesterday. Believe me, you are going to have fun doing the chute and the roller coaster. It's really fun. I'm serious. You're going to have fun. Besides, did you see how embarrassed that couple was? This is a highlight of the circuit, and not doing it is embarrassing."

"Oh, so now we're down to it, huh? It's a macho thing. *That's* what it all boils down to, isn't it?"

"When we go down the chute, everyone in the camp will line the bank. They'll cheer us on. No one cheers on someone who portages his canoe around this challenge."

"Why do they do that?"

"What? Line up to watch? It's what people do. I've seen it every time I've been up here."

"Why? Is it like people who slow down to gawk at accidents on the highway?"

"No," I argued. "You don't have the right frame of mind at all. It's more like the way people watch others on scary rides in a carnival. A vicarious thrill especially more meaningful if they themselves are in line for the ride."

"Oh, that was good," Sue laughed. "You won me over with that, you silver-tongued devil, you. Okay, I'm psyched. Let's get on this carnival ride."

*   *   *

We stood on the bank over the rocky cliff above the chute. Below us a deep whirlpool circled, water turned aside as the river pounded into the base of the cliff and divided into the main stream rushing to the right and a side current circling left into the whirlpool.

"Okay, let me walk you through this," I said. "Always remember to paddle hard and fast. The most important thing is that we stay ahead of the current. We want to control the river, not let it control us. When we reach this point," I said, aiming a finger toward the bottom of the chute, I'll yell, 'Sweep!' and you go into a sweeping stroke. I'll J-stroke, backstroke, check, whatever's necessary, to bring the bow around. Then when we're at the right angle to make this dogleg turn, "I'll yell, 'Regular stroke,' and you dig in.

"We have to make this turn," I warned. "If we don't, we end up like those beaver sticks." I pointed to several bare, gnawed sticks circling and circling in the whirlpool below.

"What happens if we *do* get trapped in there?"

"Except for people laughing at us from up here, I have no idea."

"But you have a backup plan for everything. That's one of the reasons I married you."

"That may be," I smiled, "but if we end up stuck in the whirlpool, I have no idea what we'll do."

"Well, then, I guess we'd better make the corner," she grinned.

"Once we're around the turn," I said, pointing downstream, "we need to cut across the roller coaster at a forty-five degree angle because the deep channel is on the left side. The right side is shallow and full of boulders. Unless we're having problems, you don't need to do anything different. I'll do everything from the stern. But keep paddling. Keep ahead of the current.

"Okay, Babes," I said, turning to her when she remained silent, looking at the river below, "I know you're ready, but I want to review all the strokes because you never know for sure what you're going to need on a stretch like this." Sue nodded and looked at me calmly.

"When I say 'Sweep,' what do you do?"

"I reach out as wide as I can and do broad, shallow strokes as if I were sweeping a broom just below the surface."

"Okay. I say, 'Check.' What do you do?"

"I jam my paddle straight down and hook my thumb in the side of the canoe as if I were putting on the brakes."

"Exactly. 'Switch'?"

"I switch over to the other side to paddle."

"Perfect," I praised. "Now the tricky one. What do you do if I say, 'Pray'?"

"Well," Sue laughed, "I tell you to do it yourself. If I can't get a simple thing like a little rain so that I can sleep in, I certainly can't save us in the middle of a raging river."

* * *

We were putting on our life jackets when one of the women from the Williams Lake group called down from the bank, "Are you going to run the chute now?"

"Yes," Sue answered. "We're on our way."

"I'll get your picture," she smiled, holding up a camera. "I'll send it to you if it turns out all right. Good luck! We'll be watching."

"We exchanged addresses yesterday," Sue explained as we moved the canoe into position. I held it while she made her way to the bow. Then, shoving off, I stepped over the gunnel into my place in the stern.

As we swung the canoe around the face of the campground, we could see people making their way to the bank above the chute. The word had spread.

In every marathon I've run, there has always been a moment just before the gun goes off when I've had the same thought. People around me are bouncing on their running shoes, excited, chattering, bundles of barely suppressed energy. I, on the other hand, have drawn deep into myself, knowing that in just seconds I will be swept into this crowd, carried along with no turning back. And I always ask myself, *What am I doing here?*

As Sue and I rounded the corner and entered the current that would sweep our canoe over the brink of the chute, I had this same moment of reflection. Despite all the assurances I had given her in the past couple of days, I, nevertheless, had an overwhelming sense of foreboding, a very real apprehension about being ripped forward by forces over which I had so little control. It was as if I were asking myself, *What are we doing here?*

The canoe surged forward as we entered the current leading to the lip of the chute. The bow lifted and then dropped, plunging us downward into the raging funnel of water. The cliff from which Sue and I had planned our attack shot by on the left. I was faintly aware of people lined along its edge as we streaked by.

At our predetermined point to turn into the dogleg at the bottom of the chute, I yelled, "Now, Babes. Sweep! Sweep!" She leaned forward and, reaching out as far as she could, began frantically paddling with wide, shallow strokes. At the same time, I pulled back with a strong J-stroke, leaning on the paddle to force the canoe into a sharp swing to the right.

However, I may have overcoached Sue because her sweeping strokes were almost frenzied, most of them barely skimming the surface of the water and throwing a heavy spray into my face and chest. My vision blurred as water poured down the lenses of my glasses. I stopped paddling to reach up and pull the glasses down my nose so that I could see over them.

What I saw was alarming. We had made the turn, but in the moment when I had quit paddling and Sue maintained her adrenalin-fueled sweeping, the bow had continued its swing to the right. The current was beginning to catch my side of the stern, turning us sideways to the rushing water. And once sideways to that current, we would swamp for sure.

"Switch, Babes!" I yelled. "Switch!" She immediately swung her paddle to the right side of the canoe. "Sweep!" I commanded. "Sweep!" With both of us paddling from the right, we pulled the canoe back into alignment and plunged down the river.

"Switch again!" Sue returned to her normal side, paddling right-handed while I stayed on the left-hander's side of the canoe.

"Normal stroke, Babes!" I reached out to pull hard on an exaggerated J-stroke. Then I pulled another. With the canoe knifing through the rapids at a perfect forty-five-degree angle, we cut across the roller coaster to the deep channel on the left.

"Pull, Babes! Pull. Stay ahead of the current." We pounded through the roller coaster, riding its deep swells as the river pushed us along its course between the high bank on the left and the rocky shallows on the right.

And then ahead of us, we could see a wide, deep pool created by a large log jam across the river. This pool was our takeout point for the portage around the cascades. As we neared the pool, the waves that had been carrying us along began to lose strength. The river turned from wild to tame, and we glided into the quiet pool, leaving the roar of the roller coaster behind.

We drifted for a few moments, relishing the still water. Suddenly, Sue held her paddle over her head with both hands and yelled, "That was so much fun!" She turned to face me. "That was so much fun!"

"I told you it would be," I laughed. That's what I said, but I was thinking, *Don't look down. Just don't look down.*

"Let's do it again," she bubbled.

"What?"

"Let's do it again. Let's take the canoe back up the trail and do it again. I'll bet no one has ever done it twice."

"Actually, I did see some kids do that a couple of trips ago," I answered, "but they were teenagers. We're not teenagers." *Don't look down. Don't look down.*

"Well, I feel like a teenager right now," Sue laughed, turning back to the bow. "That was so much . . ." She leaned forward, peering over the side of the canoe. Lifting a hand to shade her eyes, she stared into the depths of the pool.

I waited, but she said nothing. We paddled to the muddy takeout point and pulled the canoe through the muck to a grassy bank. Her silence continued.

I untied our boots from the middle thwart, and we carried them to a jumble of boulders, where we washed our muddy feet. Still she said nothing.

After we had dried our feet and pulled on our boots, she stood up and looked across the pool. I tried to delay the moment I had been dreading by taking my time tying my boots. Finally she spoke.

"Were those things what I thought they were?"

"What things?" I asked innocently.

"*What things*? I'll show you *what things*," she replied, roughly pulling me up by the arm.

We returned to the grassy bank. Pointing to the pool, Sue said, "*Those things.*"

"Oh," I answered, "those things."

The pool was ten to twelve feet deep and crystal clear. In a tangled pile on the muddy bottom lay a ghostly graveyard of canoes, the splintered remains of at least six or seven, all of them broken in half.

"No big deal," I assured Sue. "Those have been there my last couple of trips. I don't think there are any new ones since the last time I was here. Well," I continued, "maybe that blue one is new, but the rest have been here for at least five or six years."

"Is that supposed to comfort me?" Sue asked. "I see what could have happened to us, and I'm supposed to take comfort in the fact that it all happened a few years ago instead of yesterday?"

"That could never happen to us," I shrugged. "Those are all fiberglass. Our aluminum canoe wouldn't break in half like that."

"That's not the point," Sue fired back. "The point is the people in those canoes lost control up there somewhere, and the canoes ended up like this. If this is what happened to their canoes, I hate to think what must have happened to *them*!

"*And*," she added, pointing a finger at me, "you *knew* about these and didn't tell me."

"I still don't see the point," I replied. "Would you have felt better if you had known about them before we ran the river?"

"Maybe," she sniffed. "Maybe not. I don't know."

"Let me show you something," I said. "See how all the canoes except the blue one are the same dark forest green. And see the big numbers on some of the bows? Those are rental canoes from a lodge on Bowron Lake. That probably means these people weren't experienced enough to run this stretch of river. They couldn't handle it the way we did."

Encouraged by the lack of argument from Sue, I continued. "Think how careful we were. Before we did the run, we went over every maneuver we would need at each point in the river. Imagine what can happen to novices who just blindly plunge into the chute."

"You know what?" Sue sighed, turning her gaze from the canoes to me. "What?"

"I don't really care that you didn't tell me about those canoes. If I had known about them before we ran that stretch of river, I would have been really scared, even more scared than I already was. But now that we've run it, those canoes don't matter. Because we *did* it. And we did it absolutely perfectly."

"Well, almost perfectly," I corrected. "There was that one hairy moment coming out of the dogleg."

"We did it *perfectly*," Sue said in a measured voice that allowed no contradiction.

"You're absolutely right," I smiled. "We did it perfectly."

"You're darn right, we did." She moved closer and took my arm, turning me away from the pool. "Now if you want to put some distance between us and that crowd up the river, we'd better hit the road."

As we walked toward the canoe, she added, "By the way, I've been meaning to ask you something. Why is your shirt so wet?"

A MOSSY INTERLUDE

"It's so beautiful," Sue said in a voice I could barely hear over the roar of the waterfall. We stood on a damp mossy bank, looking up at the ledge over which Isaac River plunges thirty-five feet to a pool below. Mist rose from the pool, water swirling around and around, seeming to gather strength before rushing down the ravine to McLeary Lake below.

After leaving the takeout point at the bottom of the roller coaster, we had portaged the canoe around the cascades, a riotous stretch of rapids filled with log jams and boulders, to the bear cache where we had left our packs earlier that morning.

"Seems like yesterday instead of only a few hours ago we put those up there," Sue said from the safe distance she now always assumed whenever I climbed the ladder to a cache.

We tied in our gear and paddled for a mile before reaching the takeout point above the falls. The run down this section of Isaac was mild compared to the upper river, but it was good practice for Sue in learning to read the water. She would need that skill when we ran the Cariboo.

We carried the canoe down the steep trail to McLeary Lake, and on the return trip for our packs, we hiked a side trail to the viewpoint where we now stood beneath Isaac River Falls.

"Absolutely beautiful," Sue repeated, leaning her head on my shoulder. A breeze rustled the cedar boughs overhead, carrying their fragrance to us.

Suddenly the mood was broken by the sharp chittering of a squirrel on a limb directly above us. We looked up at his black beady eyes and quivering upper lip. "I think he's telling us something," Sue smiled.

"Right. He's telling us to get our tails out of his place. And even though I hate to agree with such an obnoxious little character, I have to admit he's right. If we're going to stay ahead of the pack, we'd better get back on the trail."

Running Isaac River

On the trail again

SWEEPERS AND DEADHEADS

"**I wish we were** staying here tonight," Sue offered as she rinsed our lunch dishes.

"I know what you mean," I replied, straightening up from the canoe, where I had tied in our backpacks. I looked across tiny McLeary Lake to the far shore, where a small cabin nestled in cedars and hemlocks. "It's one of my favorite spots on the circuit."

"Is that a patrol cabin or a shelter?" Sue asked, stepping to my side and handing me our day pack.

"A patrol cabin," I answered, leaning over the canoe to buckle in the pack. "There are two of them over there. You can't see the second one from here."

"Tell me again the difference between a patrol cabin and a shelter."

"The patrol cabins are off-limits to people doing the circuit. They're for use by Park Service personnel when they work out here. It's unusual to see two at the same location, but I suspect large crews stay here from time to time to clear hazardous debris from the river."

"And the shelters?"

"The shelters are little more than rundown huts. Some of them are cabins built by fishermen and guides over fifty years ago. Basically, they're for emergency use. People who swamp can stay in them. They have woodstoves, so people can get warm and dry out gear."

"Do they have beds?"

"They have a couple of bunks, yes."

"Do people *have* to be in trouble to use them?"

"No," I answered, "as long as they understand those in trouble come first."

"Is there one on Lanezi Lake?"

"As a matter of fact, yes. There's one in the campground where we'll probably spend tonight."

"A bed would be nice," Sue hinted.

"The problem is the sharing you'd have to do."

"Sharing? Why would we have to share? I assume they're on a first-come basis. Of course, if someone in trouble needed the shelter, we'd move out."

"I'm not talking about people. Other creatures like those shelters, too—especially mice and packrats."

"Oh," Sue answered, visibly disappointed. "Well, you might have said that right away instead of getting my hopes up."

We sat on the bank to remove our shoes and socks and roll up our pant legs, getting ready for the river. Having tied the boots to the middle thwart, I turned to Sue, who remained sitting. She was noticeably stalling.

Finally, she sighed, "Okay, I guess we're ready for our next adventure." But she made no move to stand up. She sat still, looking toward the near corner of the lake, where we would enter the Cariboo River.

I returned to a sitting position beside her and, leaning back on one elbow, suggested, "Let's go over our approach to this river one more time."

"I'm the eyes," Sue recited in a monotone. "It's a glacial river. It'll be milky, so we won't be able to see below the surface. I need to warn you of rocks, sweepers, shallow riffles, gravel bars—all that stuff."

"And deadheads," I added.

"Deadheads? What are deadheads? You haven't said anything about deadheads, whatever *those* are."

"Sure I did. Deadheads. You *have* to watch for deadheads. They're one of the most dangerous things in the river."

"You never said anything about something called a deadhead," Sue insisted, regaining some of her fire.

"Okay," I agreed, "maybe I didn't. A deadhead is a tree in the river. They're jammed into the bottom and usually stick up at an angle. Think of the pilings you see at jetties. It's as if one of those poles were pointing up at you, only usually at an angle. They're tricky because sometimes they're just below the surface. When that happens, you don't see them until you're almost on top of them."

"And those differ from sweepers, how?" Sue sniffed.

"Sweepers are trees that hang off the banks into the river, or sometimes they're completely in the water, usually hung up near the banks.

"Do I *have* to remember that distinction? Can't I just call everything a tree?"

"I suppose," I answered. "But I'll have a much clearer picture of what you see and where it is if you say 'sweeper' or 'deadhead.'"

"Okay, I'll do my best to be specific about sweepers and deadheads. Anything else I should know?"

"Well, now that you mention it. On that last stretch, you did a good job of reading the river, but when you saw a boulder or a log, you'd say, 'Rock ahead' or 'Log ahead.' The problem is I need to know *where* ahead. To the left? To the right? Straight ahead? Say things like that. 'Log straight ahead.' 'Rock on the right.' That kind of thing."

"You know," Sue said after a moment of silence, "when we came up here, you were the one who was supposed to guide us through everything. You didn't say anything about heaping this kind of responsibility on me."

I stood up and reached down to help her to her feet. "Babes, I don't want to make this sound like a life-and-death thing because it's not. Running a river like this is fun. You'll do just fine. If fact, you'll do more than fine. Remember how much fun you had running the chute and the roller coaster. Well, this is going to be like that, only not nearly so tricky."

"Yes, but then I didn't have to do anything but listen to you yell instructions to me from behind," she answered. "I wasn't yelling things back."

I put my arm around her shoulders and pulled her close. "You'll do fine."

"Of course, I'll do fine. I always do, don't I?"

"You always do."

Pulling away, Sue smiled. "Well, okay then, Kemo Sabi. What do you say we get this show on the road?"

RUNNING THE CARIBOO RIVER

The blue-green water of McLeary Lake funneled into the latte-colored rush of the Cariboo River. Paddling hard to stay ahead of the current, we began our five-mile run down this churning, twisting obstacle course.

Sue rose to the challenge as if she had been running rivers for years. "Log on the left just ahead at that bend . . . A set of ripples straight on. Goes most of the way across the channel . . . Deadhead on the right . . . Sweeper hanging out from that high bank ahead." She kept up a constant barrage of warnings as we maneuvered around one hazard after another, her reports answered in turn by my responses.

"We're going down the left channel . . . Switch, Babes . . . Sweep . . . Switch back . . . That's a false ripple. We'll go straight through it . . . Cutting across to the far side. We'll take that little chute over there . . . Okay, pull hard here. Pull hard. That's it! Good job."

When describing the river to Sue, I had emphasized the dangers of debris in the water, but I had forgotten the tricky twists and turns of the river itself. Winding its way through rocky shores and collapsing banks, the river demanded undivided attention and split-second decisions.

At one point a couple of miles into the run, Sue called back to me, "There's a tree across the river ahead. It might be blocking everything. I can't tell for sure."

"I see it," I answered, looking past her shoulder. The tree's ragged, dirt-clogged roots were still on the face of the washed-out bank below where it had stood. Because the river made a sharp turn to the left at that point, I couldn't see if the tree extended completely across it.

"We'll put in here and check it out," I told Sue, turning the canoe at an angle that would take us to a gravel bar on our right.

"We can sneak by on the left," I said a few minutes later as we stood on the bank above the tree. I pointed to the far side of the river, where the current was rushing through a narrow channel of water between the top of the tree and a rocky bank.

"Wouldn't it be safer to unload the canoe and carry everything around this?" Sue asked.

"Safer, yes . . . but necessary, no. I'm confident we have room to get through."

"Then let's do it," Sue agreed.

Ten minutes later, we swept past the tree, several feet to spare on each side of the canoe.

"Piece of cake," Sue called over her shoulder.

"Piece of cake," I agreed, pulling hard to take us back into the main current.

A short time later, a flash of white on the left bank caught my attention. A bald eagle had lifted its head from something it was eating in the rocky shallows.

"Look, Babes!" I yelled. "An eagle on the left! Right at the edge of the water!"

"I *can't* look," she answered. "I don't have time for sightseeing."

"Too late anyway," I replied, looking over my shoulder at the eagle as it returned its bloody beak to its meal.

STORMS AND DEER FLIES

"**I wish you could** have seen that eagle," I said as we sat on a rocky sand spit in the small delta where the Cariboo River emptied into Lanezi Lake.

"I do, too, but I couldn't. I made up my mind if we swamped in this river, it wouldn't be because I didn't do my job looking out for stuff."

"Well, you did a great job," I smiled.

"I know," she agreed, stretching her arms above her head. "I'm getting really good at all this."

We sat in silence looking down the lake, its surface choppy from a moderate wind blowing directly into us. The lake's color was only a couple of shades lighter than the glacial river that fed into it.

"Okay," Sue yawned. "I'm ready to hear about it."

"About what?"

"About why you think this lake hates you. Remember when we were talking yesterday? You said Lake Lanezi hates you."

"Well, I've just never had a good time on this lake," I answered. "In the first place, it's a hard lake to paddle for a couple of reasons. Even more than the other lakes, it's subject to sudden windstorms, and when the winds come, they come straight up the lake right at you. Feel that breeze in our faces right now? Makes me uneasy already, thinking the lake is plotting something.

"Also, it's hard to get off this lake when you *do* run into trouble. We have to stay to the right side because that's where the campgrounds are. But the right side is mostly rocky cliffs and rockslides from that mountain range up there." I pointed to the high peaks dominating the near side of the lake.

"So it's always stormy here?" Sue asked.

"Not always. But when the storms hit, they can last a while. The first time I did the circuit, Kip and I had to hole up on this lake for two full days because of a storm. There was no way we could move until the rains and winds finally let up.

"But I've also had trouble here on bright, sunny days. At least once with the wind again."

"You had wind on a sunny day?"

"Uh huh. The time I did the circuit solo, the sun was bright overhead, and I was cruising down the lake, thinking for once it was going to leave me alone. Suddenly, the wind came raging up the lake right into my face. Making any progress was nearly impossible. I was struggling just to hold my own, paddling into the wind the way I was."

"What did you do?"

"I moved up in the canoe, all the way to the middle thwart, to try to keep the bow down because the wind was picking it up. But all of a sudden, a gust of wind caught the underside of the bow, lifted it, turned the canoe forty-five degrees, and slammed me back down into the lake, broadside to the waves. I was looking straight over there," I said, pointing to the far side of the lake.

"You were broadside to the waves? How'd you keep from swamping?"

"I just helped the waves turn me around, and then I went back the way I had come."

"You paddled all the way back to here?" Sue laughed.

"No, before I got this far, I saw a huge pile of drift logs at the bottom of one of the ravines and managed to make my way over to it. I climbed the pile, pulling the canoe up behind me, all the way to the top."

"You pulled a fully loaded canoe to the top of a pile of drift logs?"

"Well, you have to remember I was traveling alone," I reminded her. "There was only one pack in the canoe. But it's amazing what you can do with a little rush of adrenaline."

"So you were perched on top of a pile of logs with your canoe beside you," Sue smiled. "Then what did you do?"

"I took out my book and read."

"You what?"

"I took out my book and read. It was a bright, sunny day. Just a little windy, that's all."

"How long did you stay there?"

"Oh, at least a couple of hours. I left when a canoe went by and the people in it looked at me kinda funny. I suppose I *did* look weird, sitting on that pile of logs with the canoe beside me. Anyway, when I saw them go by, I realized the wind had died down, so I pulled the canoe off the logs and went on my way."

"What else?" Sue asked.

"What do you mean, what else?"

"You said you've had trouble on sunny *days*—plural. What other kind of trouble has this lake given you on sunny days?"

"One of the hottest days I've experienced on the circuit was on this lake," I began. "I was low on water and saw a place where a small stream trickled down one of the cliffs. I managed to find a place to put in and climbed to a high point where I could fill the water jug.

"Suddenly a swarm of huge biting deer flies attacked me. And I mean *attacked* me. Their bites were like bee stings. A black, biting cloud completely engulfed me. Scrambling down the ravine, I ran for the canoe and paddled like mad all the way into the middle of the lake before I escaped them."

Sue pondered what I had said for a few moments before asking, "Remember what else you said when you told me the lake hated you?"

"I'm not sure."

"You said you knew it couldn't possibly hate *me*. That's what you said. And you know what? I think your luck on Lanezi is about to change." She stood up, stretched, and extended a hand to pull me to my feet. "You know why I think this? Because this lake *loves* me. I can feel it. So let's get on our way, big guy, because I *own* this lake."

I looked to the dark clouds rolling over the top of the mountain range. "If Lanezi Lake owes you some love," I replied, "the next couple of hours might be just the time to show it."

ATTITUDE ADJUSTMENT

Black clouds roiled overhead as we beached at the mouth of Turner Creek. The creek separated two campgrounds, one much larger than the other. We had chosen the smaller of the two.

We stretched the kinks from our backs, elbows behind us, palms above our hips. It had been a difficult paddle down the lake, the wind in our faces as we pushed through waves breaking into small whitecaps in the increasingly hostile weather.

Having the campground to ourselves, we had our choice of campsites. After we had made our selection, we returned to the canoe to unpack our gear.

"You know, Babes," I commented, reaching for the first ties in the canoe, "you have become an expert canoeist. That last stretch would have been tough for us early in the trip, but today we dug in, found perfect rhythm, and plowed right through every challenge Lanezi threw at us."

"You know what I think?" she answered. "I think when it comes to this lake, you need an attitude adjustment. It sounds to me as if you blame this lake for things that could happen on any of the lakes up here. So far I don't see anything about it that's so bad. It's nothing compared to what we dealt with yesterday on Isaac. Nope," she continued, "this lake's a pussycat, and I'm even more convinced than ever that Lanezi loves me.

"Lakes are a lot like people, I think," she continued. "Give them love, and they'll return love. Distrust them the way you distrust Lanezi Lake, and they'll earn that distrust. So loosen up, and give Lanezi a little love. Maybe, then, it'll quit picking on you."

I lifted one of the packs from the canoe, carried it to the bank, and returned for the other. Sue hadn't moved.

"Well?" she asked.

"Well what?"

"What do you think about the good advice I just gave you?"

"What I think, my dear," I answered, handing her the ax and shovel, "is that you've been reading too many women's magazines."

Sue grinned and brushed past me, carrying the ax and shovel to the bank. I followed with the second pack. After another trip for the paddles and camp stove, we carried the canoe to a safe position on the bank and overturned it for the night.

"Tell me again why you like to have our canoe clearly visible from the lake," Sue asked.

"It invites those who are looking for company and warns off those wanting privacy."

"Well, I can't imagine you wanting company," Sue grinned.

"And I can't imagine you wanting privacy," I countered.

"How come I didn't know you were a hermit before we were married?"

"How come I didn't know you were a social butterfly?"

"You *did* know," Sue answered. "That's what attracted you. Opposites attract, you know."

"Oh, that's it," I smiled. "I wondered what the attraction was."

Sue laughed and moved closer, hooking her arm through mine. "Ours, my dear, is a marriage made in heaven."

"And speaking of the heavens," I replied, looking up at the darkening sky, "we'd better get camp set up as soon as possible because, no matter how much you believe this lake loves you, all hell's going to break loose any time now."

* * *

The sky opened up just as I had finished tying our packs onto the bear cache. "This is going to last a while," I shouted over the wind as we hurried back into our campsite. "Let's duck into the tent and wait it out."

"A nap?" Sue smiled. "Okay, but I want you to know you're twisting my arm."

"Our dinner may be peanut butter sandwiches tonight," I answered, holding up a hand to shield my face from the rain as I looked upward. "Still think this lake loves you?"

"It loves me," she answered in an assured voice. "And we can't have peanut butter sandwiches because we've eaten all our bread. Remember?"

"Well, then," I replied, "our dinner tonight may be peanut butter sandwiches *without* bread."

"You know," she grinned, "sometimes you're just plain goofy."

*   *   *

Half an hour later, I lay on my sleeping bag, listening to the rain. Sue, sound asleep, was curled beside me. She had drifted off almost immediately after we had crawled into the tent and stretched out.

I turned the page in my book. I wasn't really reading, however. My mind refused to let go of the day's events. Sue had done so well. Before this trip, the closest she had come to a wilderness experience had been herding her Cub Scout troop through Portland's zoo. In the last eight hours, she had carried her pack over two portages, run two whitewater rivers and held her own in a headwind on Lanezi Lake.

I turned my head toward her. She was in a deep, quiet sleep, her breathing slow and regular, as much at peace in this Canadian rainstorm as she would have been at home in an Oregon rain.

I thumbed back to the point in my novel where my mind had wandered. *Stephen King*, I thought to myself, *now here's a guy who could really appreciate Lanezi Lake.*

FIG NEWTONS AND CANADIAN CONVERSATION

We emerged from the tent at five o'clock. A paddle striking a gunnel had alerted us to the arrival of other canoeists. The rain had stopped, but the sky was still a gloomy gray. On the sand spit, the Williams Lake people were unloading their canoes.

"See, I told you," Sue grinned. "No rain. Good company. A regular dinner." She patted me on the shoulder, condescendingly. "You, my friend, are a pessimist."

"Right," I answered, looking overhead once again at the dark clouds continuing to roll across the mountain range behind us. "But if you're looking for good company and a regular dinner around a campfire tonight, you'd better get it all in within the next hour or so."

*   *   *

Sue had been right again. The rain held off, and after dinner we prepared to join the Williams Lake group for coffee.

"Now remind me who's who," I said as I removed our container of instant coffee from the day pack. "You know how I am with names."

"Okay," she answered. "Frank is the older man, the one who does most of the talking."

"Right. I remember Frank."

"His wife is Marlene. She's the lady who's so attractive for her age."

"Okay. Marlene. Frank's wife. Attractive but old."

"Not *old*. Mature."

"Right."

"Clayton is the other man. Hardly ever says anything."

"Got it. Clayton, a Clint Eastwood type."

"Clayton's wife is Dorothy. She's Marlene's sister. Came down from Canada to attend Oregon State. Met Clayton there. He was actually born in . . ."

"Whoa! Whoa!" I interrupted. "*Way* too much information. I just want names."

"All right then. You have all the names. Run them back at me."

"There's Frank, the leader," I began, ticking off the names on my fingers. "And Claymore . . ."

"Clayton," she corrected.

"Right. Clayton. Then there's Frank's wife, Marlene, the good-looking one. And finally Doris, the not so good-looking one."

"Dorothy!" Sue corrected in an exasperated voice. "Look, you'd better forget the names and just point at them instead. Just point and grunt whenever you want into the conversation. Like the Neanderthal you are."

"Oh, oh," I smiled. "Do I detect a less-than-loving attitude here? Remember, if you *want* love, you must *give* love."

"Are you coming?" Sue asked, turning away.

"Right behind you," I replied, falling into step.

"Frank, Claymore, Marlene, and Doris," I repeated in a low voice as we approached the other camp.

"Just point," Sue said without looking back.

"Just point," I whispered. "Right. Got it." We stepped from the darkness into the warm circle of light from our hosts' welcoming fire.

*   *   *

"This is a beautiful campground," Marlene remarked, offering us a plate of Fig Newtons.

"We really shouldn't be eating your cookies," Sue protested.

"Oh, don't worry about that," Marlene smiled. "These are Frank's favorites. We always bring three times the amount we'll eat."

"Fig Newtons," Frank said, lifting his coffee cup in salute. "The only cookie that gets better with age."

"You're right about this campground, Marlene," Sue smiled, brushing crumbs from her shirtfront. "In fact, it's one of Bob's favorite campgrounds on his favorite lake. Isn't that right?" she purred, leaning into me.

"Right as rain," I agreed, looking upward.

"I'm surprised we have the place to ourselves," I continued, lowering my gaze. "I expected that crowd from Isaac Lake to arrive in force today."

"You'd think so," Frank agreed. "But as it turned out, some of them decided to stay on Isaac an extra day. And others were planning to run only one river today and camp at McLeary Lake tonight. I think everyone just wants the crowd to thin out a little and they're jockeying to find some space."

"Well, the campground on the other side of the creek can handle a lot more people than this one," I noted. "So it'll probably be a bigger draw when they *do* start showing up. Besides, it has a shelter, and that's always an attraction for some reason. I think people believe a campground with a shelter is safer or . . . I don't know . . . maybe more civilized or something."

"I think a shelter would be a nice break," Dorothy sighed.

"I thought so, too," Sue agreed, "until Bob told me the shelters have mice and packrats."

"Oh," Dorothy frowned. "So much for the shelters then."

"Hey, Clayton," I said, attempting to draw him into the conversation, "I hear you and Dorothy met at Oregon State."

"That's right," he smiled. "I'm a Canadian by choice, not by birth like these three here. In fact, I'm originally an Oregonian like you. I was born and raised in Pendleton . . ."

As Clayton talked, Sue raised a hand to her face as if rubbing her nose and whispered behind the hand, "Nice job. You got the names right."

Looking across the fire at Clayton and trying not to move my lips in my best ventriloquist imitation, I returned her whisper. "I knew the names. I was just giving you a bad time." I pulled away from the elbow I felt coming and picked up Clayton's narrative in midsentence.

" . . . no question where I was going to college. My family's all Beavers. We bleed orange and black through and through.

"Anyway, one day in the spring of my junior year, I was walking across campus when some girls came walking toward me. And in the middle of the group was this beautiful Canadian girl. Of course, at the time I didn't know she was Canadian. But I did know one of the other girls in the group, so that afternoon . . ."

"Thought you said he didn't talk much," I whispered.

"Definitely not Clint Eastwood," Sue agreed, pretending to rub her nose again.

Ten minutes later, having taken us through his courtship and marriage proposal, Clayton concluded his monologue. "And when I came up here to meet her family and saw British Columbia, I said, 'This is where I want to live the rest of my life. This truly is God's country.'"

"Hear, hear!" said Frank, raising his coffee cup in another salute. "To Canada."

"To Canada," we all joined in.

"And now you know," smiled Dorothy, patting her husband on the shoulder, "why we don't encourage Clayton to speak."

Our laughter was interrupted by hissing from the coals at the fire's edge as raindrops began splattering around us. After a quick "Thank you and see you in the morning," Sue and I hurried to our camp, barely arriving before a heavy downpour.

"Wasn't that fun?" Sue laughed as she pushed her legs into her sleeping bag. "Can you believe Clayton? It was as if a dam broke loose. Words just poured out of him."

Leaning over to kiss me on the cheek, she said, "I'm having so much fun on this trip. Thanks again for bringing me here."

"No problem," I answered, reaching up to slide my flashlight into the hanging loop above my head.

"You know," she continued, "when *you* proposed, you promised to show me the world."

"And I intend to keep that promise," I replied, maneuvering my paperback into the light. "Bowron Lakes today, Italy tomorrow."

"Italy tomorrow," Sue mused as she drifted off to sleep.

A short time later, I reached up and switched off the flashlight. I lay in the dark, listening to the rain drumming on the tent. Overhead, the trees groaned, swaying in the wind. The sides of the tent pushed in and puffed out as wind gusts toyed with it. And in only a few minutes, the storm had lulled me into sleep.

DAY 7

FUNERAL PLANS

The capriciousness of the weather on the Bowron Lake circuit could not have been better illustrated than by the sky that greeted me the next morning. I had awakened a couple of times during the night to the sounds of the storm as wind and rain hammered the campground. But when I awoke at daybreak, I needed a moment or two to recognize what was different. Silence. Everything outside the tent was silent. I pulled back the tent flap and looked out. The smell of soggy ground and dripping fir trees was a reminder of the evening's storm, but the weather had definitely taken a turn for the better. I crawled from the tent and looked toward the lake. Its surface was calm, mist floating upward toward a clear sky becoming streaky purple and orange from the rising sun.

Twenty minutes later, I was at the lake's edge, water beginning to boil in a camp kettle over our single-burner stove. I had moved the canoe a few feet to give myself some dry ground and swung it sideways to the lake. I dropped a spoonful of instant coffee into my cup. Then I leaned back against the canoe and looked out across the water.

Shadows receded to the shores as overhead an orange-yellow sky faded to pale blue. Somewhere in the distance, a loon greeted the sun with one of its mystic calls.

You know, Bob, I thought to myself, *you joke around, creating an entertaining story until you trap yourself into pretending it's really true.* I had woven a fantasy from my previous mishaps on Lanezi, personifying the lake, turning it into a plotting adversary. As a result, Sue had become a champion for Lanezi in a contest that existed only in my mind.

No, the lake didn't hate me. It had thrown more challenges at me than any other lake on the circuit, but, in doing so, it had given me more memories—more stories.

Would Sue and I remember the quiet evenings we had spent on the lakes, the times I had sipped my allotted Scotch and she had leaned into me as we marveled at magnificent multicolored sunsets? Would we remember the moose and its calf at the end of Indianpoint Lake, our foray into middle-aged skinny-dipping on Isaac, the minks' mating dance for us in the late afternoon sun?

Sure, we would. But would those moments be the gist of our stories to others? No. We would recount the naked Germans, the dropped pack ripping open Sue's head, the bear on the sand spit, the storm blowing us down Isaac Lake. Those would be the gist of our stories to others. On each of my previous trips, Lanezi had added another such story to my catalogue of man-versus-nature narratives.

I poured boiling water into my cup and settled back against the canoe once more. *I so love it up here,* I thought to myself as I sipped the steaming coffee.

Across the lake, I caught movement against the shore. A canoe drifted slowly down the lake, two people barely touching the surface with their paddles as they trolled for fish, their rods bending against the pull of the water. *We must have some early risers in the other campground,* I reflected.

Their voices carried to me as they conversed casually, occasionally working their lines against the pull of Lanezi's current. I was struck with the memory of one of my favorite passages in *Huckleberry Finn.* As Huck and Jim float down the Mississippi, Huck remarks upon their ability to pick up snatches of conversations from people half a mile across the river. *If anyone knew how sound carries across water, it would be Mark Twain,* I smiled to myself.

"Mind if I join you?" interrupted a voice from behind me. I turned to find Sue standing there, her empty cup dangling from a forefinger.

"Are they catching anything?" she asked a few minutes later, blowing cooling breath across her coffee as she studied the canoe on the other side of the lake.

"Not that I can see. But I don't know why they think they have to go clear over there. The mouth of this creek," I thumbed to my right, "is one of the best bets on the lake. It's swollen from that rain last night, so you can bet it's full of tasty little tidbits washing into the lake right now. Nope, this is the place to find fish today."

"And you want to fish it, don't you?" Sue smiled, bringing her coffee to her lips.

"Uh huh," I answered, nodding.

"But I suppose," she continued in a resigned voice, looking up at the sky, "you want to take advantage of this weather to keep our lead on the crowd coming down from Isaac Lake."

"This isn't a race," I replied. "First one finished doesn't get a prize. The point of the circuit is to *enjoy* the circuit."

"Meaning?" Sue asked, hopefully.

"Meaning I think we should take a break here. Take advantage of the good weather to dry out our gear and air out the tent."

"And go fishing?" Sue grinned.

"Well, that, too," I admitted.

"You and I are so meant for each other," Sue laughed. "When I saw the sky this morning, I said to the Man upstairs, 'Please let Bob decide to take a break today.' I'm tired after yesterday. I'd really love to take a day off."

"Let's do it then. We'll hang out here for the day. Get a few chores done, and then kick back and enjoy the sun."

"Kick back and enjoy the sun," Sue repeated. "You sure know the way to a girl's heart."

For the next few minutes, we sat silently watching the canoe across the lake as the two fishermen worked that far stretch of water. Finally, Sue broke the silence. "It's the lake, isn't it?" she asked.

"What?"

"You're in such a relaxed, good mood. I think Lanezi Lake has worked its charm on you."

"Well, now that you mention it," I began, seeing this as an opening to bring the Lanezi-Lake-hates-me thing to a close, "I think I *have* reached a better understanding of the lake on this trip."

"I *knew* it!" she exclaimed. "I knew I could bring you and Lanezi Lake together."

"Well, I think you have," I answered, almost enjoying her sense of triumph as much as she was. "I really do."

"This lake is perfect for you," Sue went on. "You're both stubborn, competitive, temperamental. I knew once you recognized the two of you were more alike than different, you'd accept each other."

Not sure whether or not that was a compliment, I merely nodded.

"You know what I've decided?" she asked. "I've decided that when you die, I'm going to cremate you, bring your ashes up here, and sprinkle you on Lanezi. It'd be the perfect coming together of you two."

"What makes you think you're going to outlive me?"

"Well, that's a given, isn't it?"

"I suppose," I agreed. "But I plan to live another fifty years. Won't you be a little old to make this trip?"

"Oh, I'm sure I can find some nice young man willing to help me," Sue smiled.

"Probably. But there are still a couple of things wrong with your plan. First, I don't *want* to be cremated. Second, I'm assuming from what you've said, you believe once sprinkled on Lanezi Lake, I'll *stay* on Lanezi Lake. The truth is, with the currents out there, I'll soon be back in the Cariboo River, then on down to Sandy Lake, and, through that, into the river again. Two miles later I'll be going over eighty-foot-high Cariboo Falls."

"I see what you mean. Probably won't be much of you left at that point, will there?"

"Well," I shrugged, "if you begin with nothing but a pile of ashes, there won't be much of me to start with."

"I guess you're right," Sue grinned. "Maybe I'd better give this a little more thought."

"No rush," I answered. "You have fifty years to think it through."

"Right," Sue replied, rising to her feet. "How about another leisurely pancake breakfast?"

"Sounds good," I nodded.

A BACKPACK ATTACK

"**They're nice people,**" Sue said as we watched the Williams Lake group paddle away from us on their way down the lake.

Our breakfast had been interrupted by Marlene, who had stopped by to tell us they were heading out. Carrying plates of half-eaten pancakes, Sue and I had accompanied her to the lake to see them off.

"Well, aren't they?" Sue demanded in answer to my silence.

"Oh, sure they are. And you know what? I'd give anything for one of their canoes."

"Right," Sue laughed. "If you owned one of those wooden canoes, we'd have to *rent* a canoe for this trip."

"What do you mean?"

"Look at the way you baby your aluminum canoe. 'Don't drag it across gravel,'" she continued, dropping into what she called my "teacher's voice." "'Don't step into it until it's in the water.' 'Always leave it bottom-side up on dry land.' You have all these rules for your aluminum canoe. Imagine what you'd be like with a fancy wooden canoe.

"Why, you'd be scared to death to bring a canoe like that up here. It might get scratched. No, if you owned one of those, it'd be in the garage while your car sat outside. You'd spend all your time waxing it or polishing it or whatever you do to wooden canoes, and you'd probably never put it in the water."

"I don't think I'd be *that* bad, but you're probably right. I might not want to bring a beauty like that up here."

"*Probably* right? You *know* I'm right. Look at how obsessive you are with *this* canoe. Actually, there are times when I think you love it more than you love me."

"Now *that's* not true. I love you just as much as I love my canoe."

"Oh, you do, huh?" Sue grinned. "Well, it's reassuring to know I'm on equal footing with a canoe."

"Yes, it is," I agreed, stooping to rinse my plate and fork in the lake. "And I want you to know," I continued, rising from the water's edge, "that, like my canoe, I'll never drag you across gravel, and I'll always leave you bottom-side up on dry land."

"You're so good to me," Sue laughed.

"Yes, I am," I replied.

"But you know what?" I continued. "Right now we need to get back to camp. We left the food pack and dirty cookware by the fire pit. Not a smart thing to do."

"Bears?" Sue asked. "You're worried about bears, aren't you? I thought you said the bears on this side of the circuit weren't a problem."

"No, I did *not* say that. I said the bears on this side aren't as aggressive. But that doesn't mean we can just ignore their presence. Tempt them, and you'll have trouble. We're going to be as careful in this second stretch as we were on the first."

"Okay, then," she answered. "Let's go."

*　　*　　*

Our campsite was undisturbed, and we spent the next hour in a camper's version of household chores. Sue heated water for the dishes, and I pulled the sleeping bags from the tent and took them to the lakeside, where I draped them inside out over the canoe to air.

Back at camp I removed the fly from the tent and spread it over some nearby brush to dry. Then I tied back the tent flaps, allowing a flow of fresh air inside.

The sun was already hot on our backs whenever we emerged from the shade of the trees, and we were eager to wrap up these tasks and take our books to a nice little beach we had spotted near the mouth of the creek.

"I'll put the packs in the bear cache, and then we can go on down to the lake," I said to Sue as she dried the last of the dishes.

"Not just yet. I want to wash out a few things. I have mine ready, so if you have some socks or other stuff you want washed, add it to my pile. But I'm afraid I need another pot of water to heat. Mind getting me it for me?"

"No problem," I replied.

*   *   *

When I returned from the creek, Sue was standing at the near side of our campsite. She held a finger to her lips and motioned me toward her. I instinctively began tiptoeing as I moved forward.

"What is it?" I whispered. "A bear?"

"No. It's something else," she answered, also whispering.

"Something else? What?"

"I don't know."

"Well," I demanded in my normal voice. "Can you at least give me a hint?"

"Come here," she continued to whisper as she turned and tiptoed into the campsite.

She stopped near the fire pit, holding up her hand. Then she pointed toward the food pack. "See anything funny?" she asked.

I looked at the pack in its place by the tent. "No," I answered.

"Well, it's not doing it now."

"Doing what?"

"I decided to put some lunch in the day pack in case we wanted to eat on the beach, but when I started to get into the food pack, it moved."

"It what?"

"It moved. It started jumping around."

"What?"

"It *moved*! I know that sounds weird, but it started quivering and moving around."

"You're kidding, right?"

"I'm serious," Sue insisted. "I knelt down to open the . . . Look! Look! It's doing it again!"

At first I saw nothing. I had started to turn back to Sue, grinning at what I now assumed was her idea of a joke, when a definite movement from the pack caught my eye. I stared. There it was again. And again.

No, Sue wasn't putting me on. But her description had been only partially correct when she said the food pack was moving. The pack itself wasn't moving. However, something inside it was.

I walked slowly toward the pack, stooping along the way to pick up a peeled beaver stick someone had carried into the camp from the creek or the lake. As I neared, the movement stopped. Kneeling, I reached out and prodded the pack with the stick. A scurrying movement inside and then stillness. I prodded it again. No movement.

Oh, man, I thought, *I'm going to have to do it.* Leaning forward and using the stick to lift the top flap, I flipped it open. Nothing. I duckwalked closer and, leaning forward, peered into the pack. At first I didn't see anything in the food packets. But when I poked the lower side of the pack, a face popped into view. Black beady eyes over a twitching whiskered nose. Rounded, cupped ears. "Oh," I called back to Sue, "It's only a . . ." But at the sound of my voice, the mouse leaped straight for my face.

I fell backward into a sitting position, my hands instinctively up to protect my face, and the mouse, with a move that would have made Michael Jordan proud, changed direction in midair, ricocheted off my left shoulder, and hit the ground running. I heard a squeal from behind me and looked over my shoulder to see Sue disappearing into the woods, the mouse racing directly behind on the same trail.

At that moment a rustling from the pack made me turn back. Like a little volcano belching out mice, the pack rocked as one mouse after another erupted from its interior, gray-brown bodies flying in all directions.

Then, as suddenly as the pandemonium had begun, it ended. I waited in the silence, watching the pack for more mouse activity. When I was sure no more would appear, I scooted around toward the path Sue had taken and waited for her return.

Finally, she emerged from the trees, walking carefully and looking around as if she expected another mouse attack at any moment. As I watched her approach, I tried to stifle a low chuckle. Laughing at this moment would not be the thing to do, and I tried hard to hold back. But the memory of her running into the woods, chased by the mouse, flooded my mind, and I couldn't help myself. I rolled to my side, holding my stomach and roaring with laughter.

"What's so funny?" Sue demanded, already grinning, caught up in the infectiousness of my laughter.

"You never cease to amaze me," I began, wiping tears from my eyes. "Two days ago you went nose to nose with a bear and didn't even flinch. But today you run screaming into the forest at the sight of a mouse?"

"Well, first of all," Sue answered, "I didn't scream. I might have yelped a little, but I didn't scream. And, second, at least a mouse didn't knock *me* on my butt."

"Good point," I grinned.

"And I want you to know," she said, sensing that she had at least partially regained the upper hand, "I *wasn't* running from that mouse. We just happened to be going in the same direction." She walked the rest of the way across the camp and took a playful swipe at my head before sitting down beside me.

"Do you think they're all out of there?" Sue asked, pointing to the pack.

"I'm *pretty* sure," I replied. "We'll find out when we empty it to assess the damage they've done."

"*We?* You don't think I'm going anywhere near that thing while there's a chance some are still in there, do you?"

"No, you just sit here and rest while I do it," I answered, rising to my feet. "You're probably tired from that long run you just finished."

*　　*　　*

"Not too bad," I concluded ten minutes later, looking at the food packages laid out before me. "They seem to have been mostly attracted to the Top Ramen you rescued from the French couple."

"I'm good with that," Sue answered. "I'd rather the mice had it than those two, anyway."

"Me, too," I agreed, as I began repacking the supplies. "Now let's get our chores done. I don't know about you, but I hear that little beach calling our names."

TWO BROTHERS AND A CHIPMUNK

An hour later, our laundry festooning low-lying brush, Sue and I lay on the beach, curling our toes in the sun-warmed sand.

"You know," I said, rolling to my side to face her with my head propped in one hand, "those mice in the pack remind me of an incident with a chipmunk that happened to my brother and me when we were teenagers."

"Really," Sue responded without opening her eyes.

"Uh huh. You want to hear about it?"

"Wait a minute," Sue answered, rolling to her side to face me. "I think I know this story. Does it begin 'Two brothers and a chipmunk enter a bar'?"

"Do you want to hear the story or not?"

"Okay," she smiled, returning to her original position and closing her eyes. "Tell me about your brother and the chipmunk."

"We hiked into North Fork of the Clackamas River," I began. "We planned to camp a few days and do some fishing. Of course, in those days we didn't have fancy freeze-dried food. We'd just toss some baloney and a loaf of bread into a pack with jars of mayonnaise and mustard, and maybe a bottle of ketchup."

"Hold it," Sue interrupted. "You took mayonnaise on a backpack trip."

"Yeah, we never worried about salmonella in those days. If you'd said *salmonella* to us, we'd probably think you were talking about a steelhead run. But you know what? We never got sick either. Sometimes I think people get sick by stressing out about getting sick."

"Interesting medical theory," she grinned.

"Anyway," I continued, "the first morning we took out the bread to make some toast, and . . ."

144

"Wait a second. You had a toaster in your pack? Where'd you plug it in?"

"You don't really want to hear this story, do you?" I snapped.

"Of course, I do," Sue smiled, turning to face me again. "It's just getting good."

"Well, when we took out the loaf of bread, something had eaten a tunnel right through it from one end to the other. Right through the cellophane wrapping at one end, through the loaf, and out the cellophane wrapping at the other end. You could hold it up and look through it like a telescope."

"I assume the culprit was the chipmunk of this story. But how'd you know it was a chipmunk?"

"The hole was just the right size. Maybe it was a small squirrel, but Jerry and I figured it was a chipmunk."

"How'd you know it wasn't a mouse or a small rat?"

"There aren't any mice or rats in the Oregon woods," I sniffed.

"Why not? There are mice up here. Why not down there?"

"I don't know. I just never saw any. When I worked for the Forest Service, we'd run across them in the outbuildings of our lookouts and guard stations, but I never saw any in the open woods. The ones in our pack today probably came from the shelter across the creek."

"Doesn't make sense to me," Sue argued. "If they aren't native to the woods, how do they get into the shelters?"

"Beats me. Maybe they arrive in tiny canoes."

"Tiny canoes," Sue mused. "I like that." She drifted off, caught up in whatever picture was going through her head.

Just when I thought she had lost the thread of my story, she broke the silence. "So, anyway, what'd you and Jerry do for food since all you brought was stuff for sandwiches?"

"Oh, we ate the bread."

"What? Ick! You ate something covered with chipmunk saliva?"

"Well, to tell you the truth, we didn't think about chipmunk spit. But we did worry about hair and other stuff he might have left behind, so we carved around the holes in the bread slices. Made them a little bigger. The sandwiches were kinda funny looking, though."

Smiling, Sue shook her head and lay back once more. She had just closed her eyes when I asked, "Did I ever tell you that on my solo trip up here I left my pack in a bear cache while I carried the canoe over a portage and when I returned, I found a big crow sitting on the pack, sorting through all my food?

"Crows might be the smartest animals in the woods, you know. That crow had untied the flaps and unzipped every zipper. He was pulling out packages, pecking holes through the wrappings, testing the food, and dropping anything he didn't like to the ground below."

When Sue didn't respond, I continued, "He seemed to hate peas. There was a pile of them under the tree."

Sue continued to ignore me. "Do you want to hear the story?" I asked.

"Didn't I just hear it?" she answered without opening her eyes.

"Oh, that was just the bare-bones outline. I can flesh it out with really fantastic details."

"You know what I really want?" Sue asked, sitting up. "I want you to go fishing."

"What?"

"I want you to go fishing. I would like to take a nap in this nice warm sun on this nice sandy beach. You, on the other hand, are obviously in a story-telling mood, and while I normally love your stories, at the moment I really need a nap. So I want you to go fishing."

"Okay," I replied, standing up and dusting sand from the back of my pants. "If that's what you want."

"Take my word for it," Sue answered, lying back down. "That's exactly what I want."

*   *   *

I want you to go fishing," I thought to myself as I returned to the campground to pick up my fishing gear. *How many husbands would give their eyeteeth to hear their wives say that? Is this a wonderful marriage, or what?*

AN ERNEST HEMINGWAY PHOTO OP

Sorting through my small assortment of lures, I knelt on a stretch of gravel at the mouth of the creek. "Anything with red on it," Larry had advised four days ago on Isaac Lake. And judging by the twelve-inch trout he had landed just before he gave me that advice, I probably should have listened to him. Instead, I played a hunch and, selecting a small silver spinner, clipped it to my line.

Though the creek was swollen from the storm, its blue-gray water still contrasted with the glacial latte of Lanezi. I could clearly distinguish the creek's flow as it fanned into the lake.

Having cast to the far edge of the stream, I used its current to carry my lure into the lake. Then I began a measured retrieve, drawing the spinner at a forty-five-degree angle through the mix of stream and lake water. Suddenly, the tip of my rod pulled violently downward as something slammed into my lure. I instinctively set the hook, jerking the rod upward to my left shoulder. I held it there, waiting for the fish to begin its run. But the line didn't move. I pulled back a little more. The line stretched tighter with no give at the other end. *Oh, no,* I thought to myself, *I'm snagged. Probably a log.*

Hoping to gain some slack and use the current to work my spinner loose, I lowered the rod, pointing its tip toward the lake's surface. But another sudden hard pull almost jerked the rod from my hands. Something flashed in the murky water before streaking for the deeper recesses of the lake.

"Definitely not a log!" I exclaimed, adjusting the drag on my reel as I applied pressure to turn the fish before I ran out of line.

* * *

Twenty minutes later, I climbed the bank and made my way to the beach where I had left Sue. I expected to find her asleep but, instead, found her reading, holding her book upward to shade her eyes from the sun. I walked across the sand, my fishing rod in my left hand, my right hand behind my back.

"Oh, hi," Sue greeted me. "Are you just going fishing?"

"No, actually I'm done fishing for the day."

"Done? You're quitting so soon?"

"Yes, I am."

"Okay," Sue began, sitting up. "I'll admit I asked you to go fishing just to get rid of you for a while. I mean, I love you and all that, but you have to agree you were being a bit difficult. You knew I wanted to nap, but you just kept running off at the mouth."

"Well, you aren't napping, after all, are you?"

"No," Sue agreed, "I'm not. Maybe I felt guilty, but I couldn't fall asleep, so I took the opportunity of the peaceful silence after you left to really get into my book. Anyway, I wasn't just trying to get rid of you." She thought a moment. "Okay, maybe I *was* really trying to get rid of you, but I still liked the idea of your going fishing."

"Why was my going fishing a good thing?"

"I'm surprised I'm saying this," Sue began, "because I've never really liked fish, but the idea of a dinner of *any* fresh food sounds great. I'm so tired of freeze-dried food. I was hoping maybe you'd catch something, and we could have a nice dinner tonight."

"How about a nice lunch instead?"

"Like what?" Sue pouted. "Freeze-dried macaroni and cheese?"

"No, I was thinking more of something like this." I brought my right hand out from behind me, holding up a cord from which dangled a large, beautifully marked fish.

"Wow!" Sue exclaimed, throwing her book aside and scrambling to her feet. "Wow!" she repeated as she came toward me. "But you just left here. How could you catch something so fast?"

"First cast," I laughed. "This fish was just waiting for me."

"It's so *big*!" Sue marveled. "What is it, a salmon?"

"No, I think it's a Dolly Varden. I've never seen one in real life, but I've seen pictures, and I think that's what it is. See these red and orange spots along its side? As far as I know, those aren't found on any other type of trout."

"So it's a trout?"

"Well, some people say it's a char, and that's a put-down for something that aspires to be a trout. But as of today, I'm claiming Dolly Vardens *are* trout because that makes this the biggest trout I've ever caught, and I've fished for them all my life."

"I'm so proud of you," Sue smiled, putting an arm around me. "I wish we had a tape measure so we could officially document your catch."

"Oh, don't worry," I replied, holding up my hand. "I have an accurate measuring device right here. My hand is exactly six inches from the base of my palm to the tip of my little finger. Let's see . . ." I laid my hand at the tail of the fish, moved it up for a second measure, and moved it up once again. "Eighteen inches to this point, "I announced, "with two more inches to go. This," I grinned, "is a twenty-inch trout. Definitely a record for me."

"Then we need some pictures," Sue smiled. "The camera's in the day pack. I'll get it."

After several Hemingway-styled poses, my fishing rod in my left hand, the Dolly Varden held toward the camera to make it appear even bigger, Sue finally decided she had adequately recorded this catch for posterity.

"So why lunch instead of dinner tonight?" she asked, returning the camera to the pack. "I'm as anxious as you are, but really a nice dinner by the fire would be a good way to end the day."

"Think back to the Seattle group with all those fish lying around their camp," I reminded her. "Remember what happened to them that night? You know what I think about taking bears lightly. No, we eat this fish right now. We don't keep it around the rest of the day."

"Can we eat all this in one meal?"

"We'll give it our best shot. And I don't know about you, but when it comes to eating, my best shot is pretty impressive."

*   *   *

I had just gutted the Dolly Varden and was about to cut off its head when Sue announced from the bank above me, "Canoe coming. I think it's Stan and Larry." I looked up the lake. Sue was right. The two men paddled with the smooth synchronized strokes of people who have canoed together for years.

I stood up as they drew near. Pointing to my rod propped against a log near me, Larry yelled, "How's the fishing?"

"Not too bad," I answered, bending to hook a finger in the gills of the trout and hold it up.

"That's a beaut," Stan called. "I gotta get a closer look at that."

"It's easier to put in at the beach," I suggested. "Pretty rocky here."

As they began a wide turn that would take them back to the beach, I knelt by my fishing rod, unclipped the silver spinner, and slipped it into my shirt pocket. I glanced at Sue, who looked puzzled. Touching my finger to my lips, I whispered, "I'll explain later."

"Let's see that thing up close," Stan said as the two of them began stepping down the bank.

"Now that's a nice Dolly Varden," Larry complimented. I looked past his shoulder to Sue, who nodded, smiling. "So did you use a lure with red on it?"

"Yeah, I did," I lied. Again I glanced at Sue, whose smile turned to a frown. "Thanks for the tip."

"I knew it," Larry grinned. "I've fished these lakes for four years straight. I know them like the back of my hand. I know what works up here."

"We're about to eat this fish for lunch," I said. "There's plenty to go around. Why don't you two join us?"

Stan shook his head. "Thanks for the offer, but that gang from Isaac Lake is behind us, and we want to beat them to the shelter in the other campground. We figure staying in it will give us a chance to dry out our gear from last night's storm."

"And speaking of last night," Larry interrupted. "You two camped here?"

When we nodded, he asked, "How'd that go?"

"What do you mean, 'How'd it go?'" I replied.

"Oh, I don't know," he answered with an amused glance at Stan. "I just thought your sleep might have been bothered somehow. It happens up here once in a while."

"Well, the storm woke us up a couple of times, but other than that, we slept just fine."

"Oh, yeah, the storm," Stan said. "I imagine *everything* hunkered down in that." He turned his face to the blue, cloudless sky overhead. "Should be clear tonight, though. Different from last night. Don't you think so, Larry?"

"Yep," Larry grinned, "probably be different tonight."

"Anyway, we have to get going if we're gonna get the shelter," Stan said. "Tell you what. If you set out before we do tomorrow morning, stop in for coffee. We'd like to hear about your night. Wouldn't we, Larry?"

"Yep, we sure would."

"And if we leave before you come by, we'll swing back over here to see how it went. Won't we, Larry?"

"Yep," Larry grinned, "we sure will."

"Those two are up to something," I said to Sue a few minutes later as we watched them paddle away.

"I know," she agreed, moving closer and putting her arm around my waist. "You don't think they're planning to sneak back over here and scare us or something, do you?"

I shook my head. "They're playful, but they aren't childish. I just think they know something we don't know. And whatever it is, they're getting a big kick out of it."

A LAID-BACK VISITOR

"Umm," Sue muttered around a forkful of trout. "So good. This is so good."

I carried the frying pan to her and scooped another piece of the fish onto her plate.

She looked up. "So tell me why you didn't want Larry to see your lure, which, by the way, *didn't* have any red on it. And why did you fib about that?"

"I was being nice," I replied. "He told me to use red, and when he thought his tip worked, look how happy it made him."

"How'd you know he'd feel like that?"

"He's a fisherman. Never tell a fisherman he's wrong when he trusts you enough to give you a tip. Telling a fisherman his tip doesn't work is like telling him his dog is ugly. It's just not done."

"I tell *you* your dog is ugly all the time," Sue replied, referring to Sarge, my saggy-faced basset hound.

"I know you do," I grinned. "I've been meaning to talk to you about that."

* * *

In the midafternoon, Sue and I began putting our camp back into order. I retrieved the sleeping bags from the canoe, and she set out to pluck our laundry from the brush where we had draped it to dry.

I was in the tent, laying out the sleeping bags when Sue threw back the flap. "Come on!" she yelled. "You've got to see this!"

She was halfway across the campground before I managed to crawl from the tent. Jumping from one foot to the other in her excitement, she motioned me on. "Come on! Hurry up before he gets away!"

She turned in the direction I was to follow, took a few steps, and then pivoted and raced back past me toward the tent. "I forgot the camera," she shouted as she streaked by. Dropping to her knees, she dove into the tent, emerging almost immediately, and ran by me again, the camera in hand.

I followed her to a stand of scrub brush along the trail to the lake, where she crouched and, lifting her head, studied something at the far side of the bushes. Holding a finger to her lips with one hand and motioning me to follow with the other, she crept forward.

A few more steps, and she dropped to one knee. I moved to a position beside her. Reaching up, she grabbed my arm and pulled me down. "You see him?" she whispered, pointing to a windfall propped at a forty-five-degree angle against a larger sun-bleached log.

"I don't see anything," I answered, also whispering.

"Right there," she insisted, jabbing her finger at the windfall.

"Where? What am I looking for?"

Right *there!*" she repeated. "How can you not see him?"

And then I did. Sitting nonchalantly on the trunk of the tree was a large yellow-brown clump of bristly hair and quivering quills.

"Oh, yeah," I said in my normal voice as I rose to a standing position. "That's a porcupine."

"Shh," Sue hushed. "I *know* it's a porcupine. Get back down here before you scare him away."

"It's not going anywhere," I replied, ignoring her tugging at my pants leg. "Porcupines don't scare easily—especially a porcupine as big as this one. And if one does feel threatened, it doesn't run away. It just hunkers down and pops up those quills on its back and tail. The quills on the back are for protection," I continued, "but the tail is an offensive weapon. If a porcupine can smack a predator in the face with its tail, a snout full of quills delivers a valuable lesson about messing with porcupines."

Sue slowly rose beside me. "Does he know we're here?" she asked in a low voice, no longer whispering but still testing whether or not our conversation would disturb the porcupine.

"Probably. They have weak eyesight, but their hearing and ability to smell are excellent. Still, whether or not they know we're around isn't always easy to say. They're pretty laid-back creatures. Leave them alone, and they'll just meander on about their business."

"And he's a big one?" Sue asked.

"Biggest I've ever seen. That thing must weigh twenty-five, thirty pounds."

"Good." She beamed. "It's only fitting that on the day you catch the biggest trout in your life, *I* find a trophy porcupine."

"*Trophy*? Well, that's hardly a word people would use for a porcu . . ." But then I caught myself as I saw Sue's smile disappear. "No, I take that back. *Trophy* is *exactly* the word I'd use for this monster."

"Right," she grinned. "And he's *my* monster. Now, I want some pictures." She snapped a couple from her present position and then, turning sideways, threaded her way through the brush a few more steps. In response to the clicking of the camera, the porcupine slowly swung its head around and stared at her.

"Look. He sees me now. He really doesn't care, does he?" Sue laughed. She took another step toward the tree. As she did, the quills on the porcupine's back lifted slightly and settled as if brushed by a breeze. But there was no breeze.

"I believe that's close enough, Babes."

"One more," she replied and snapped another picture before returning to my side.

"He's so cute," she purred.

"Cute? You call my dog ugly, and you call a porcupine *cute*?"

"Well, he *is*! Look at those button eyes and that pug nose. He's like a cuddly stuffed toy."

"Cuddly? Now cuddling with a porcupine's something I wouldn't advise."

"Why not?" Sue grinned. "After all," she added, reaching to my face and running her hand over my seven-day stubble, "I cuddle with you, don't I?"

THE GIRL AND THE FISH

That evening as we sat by our fire, allowing it to burn down before putting it out for the night, our conversation lapsed into silence. Sue leaned into me for warmth and stared into the coals.

"Tired?" I asked.

"No," she answered. "Content. This was really a nice day. Sunbathing on a remote beach, eating a beautiful trout lunch, finding a trophy porcupine—quite a day for a city girl."

I leaned forward and stirred up the fire, sending spiraling sparks into the darkness of the trees overhead. "You're not a city girl anymore, Babes. You've handled this trip so well—so much better than I could have ever imagined."

"Really!" Sue replied. "You didn't think I was tough enough?"

"Oh, I knew you were tough enough," I objected. "I just wasn't sure you'd like the trip as much as I like it."

"Well, I'm not certain I do," she admitted. "Oh, I like it well enough. Everything is so challenging, so demanding. And I know I've grown leaps and bounds. But like it as much as you do? No, probably not. I've liked it all right. But you *love* it. I'm not sure I could ever say I love it."

"That's okay," I grinned. "I'm not sure I could ever say I love an afternoon shopping in downtown Portland."

"Then that makes us even," Sue smiled.

The fire had almost burned out, and I was just about to suggest we turn in when Sue said, "There's something I was going to ask you this afternoon, but we were sidetracked by the arrival of Larry and Stan."

"And what was that?"

"How come the trout you caught today is called a Dolly Varden? I mean, isn't that a weird name for a fish?"

"You're right," I agreed. "It *is* a strange name for a fish—especially a trout. Trout and salmon have names like rainbow, German brown, Eastern brook. And there are the macho names like cutthroat,steelhead, sockeye, king, and Chinook. I mean, those are *tough* names. So why Dolly Varden for this fish?" Sue waited out my dramatic pause.

"Dolly Varden is a character in a Charles Dickens novel," I continued. "She's flirtatious and colorful. Especially known for her flashy clothing. And one of her favorite dresses is green with pink polka dots. A fashionable dress of the time was actually called a 'Dolly Varden.'"

"Oh, okay! Now I get it!" Sue exclaimed. "Some of those spots along the side *were* more pink than red. And the back of the fish *did* have a green tint."

"Well, I think the spots are more red and orange and the back of the fish more gray than green, but, anyway, that's how the trout came to be called the Dolly Varden."

"That's a great story," Sue laughed. And I'll bet you've been waiting all afternoon to tell it to me, haven't you?"

"Why would you think that?"

"Because it gave you the perfect opportunity to put on your English-teacher face and tell me a fish tale with a literary twist. That's why."

Smiling, she used my shoulder to push herself to a standing position. "Oh, don't get the wrong idea. I loved it. Dolly Varden, the girl, and Dolly Varden, the fish. It was a perfect bedtime story to end a perfect day."

"Time for bed?" I asked, coming to my feet.

"Time for bed," she yawned, taking my arm and turning toward the tent.

Nice fish. Ugly shorts.

SOUNDS THAT GO CRUNCH IN THE NIGHT

I woke in the dead of the night, disoriented by the blackness inside the tent. A few moments passed before I was able to focus on what had awakened me. Loud munching, crunching, grinding, chewing sounds outside the tent. I raised my head, listening.

"Are you awake?" Sue asked from the darkness.

I nodded and then, realizing she couldn't see me, answered, "Yes. How long you been awake?"

"Ten minutes or so. I was just about to shake you."

"And it was out there when you woke up?"

"Uh huh. What do you think it is?"

"I don't know."

"What do you mean, you don't know? You're supposed to know everything about everything up here."

"Sorry. I don't have a clue what's going on out there. I've never heard anything like this before."

"Okay," Sue answered in a calm voice. "Are you going out there and find out what's going on?"

"No."

"No? You *have* to. Something outside our tent is eating something else outside our tent. When it's through with that, what's to say we won't be next?"

"It's pitch-black outside. If I go out there, not only will I not be able to see a thing, but I very well may become dessert."

"Take the flashlight," she commanded.

"No good," I answered. "After you fell asleep when I was reading, the flashlight dimmed and then went out. The batteries are dead, and the extra batteries are in the bear cache."

"So, you're just going to lie here, listening to this thing eat whatever it's eating and take a chance on whether or not it decides to eat us?"

"Unless you have a better answer, that's exactly what I'm going to do."

"Well, I can't go to sleep under those conditions," Sue snapped.

"Then I guess we're *both* just going to lie here wide awake and wait this thing out."

But the munching, crunching, grinding, chewing sounds proved hypnotic. And eventually both of us fell sound asleep.

DAY 8

A MORNING DISCOVERY

I woke at predawn and lay still, listening to the silence outside the tent. No chewing. No gnawing. Silence. Whatever had been there during the night was gone. Or maybe not. But at least it had quit eating.

I struggled from my sleeping bag and slowly unzipped the front of the tent. Cautiously, I peeked through the opening and then crawled halfway out. Still on my hands and knees, my lower body inside the tent like a turtle ready to pull in its head at the first sign of danger, I surveyed our campsite. No movement. No rustling in the brush. Nothing.

Pulling my clothes and boots from the tent, I dressed as quickly as possible. The air in the predawn hour was cold, still heavy with the dampness of the night. My breath steamed, fogging my glasses, and I shivered as I began searching for signs of our nighttime visitor in the trees and brush along the fringes of the camp. But I found nothing.

Having returned to our campsite, I brought the packs down from the bear cache, fished out a box of waterproof matches, and made my way to the pile of firewood I had covered with a tarp the night before. Wrestling the ladder to the bear cache and hauling down the packs had momentarily warmed me, but I knew we'd need a good fire on this cold morning. A good fire and a warm breakfast before we packed up and set off down the lake.

As I approached our fire pit with my armload of dry wood, I suddenly stopped, puzzled. I relish a tidy camp. Probably to a fault. The night before, I had done what I always do: put out the fire with dirt and water, mound the scorched remains, and soak the ground around the fire pit. The scene before me violated all my principles of a well-kept camp. Our fire pit had been ransacked. Charred, partially burned firewood had been dragged from the pit and scattered across the ground.

I knelt, studying the mucky, ash-covered remains of the fire. Returning to my feet, I circled through the tangled debris that had been dragged from the pit, studying both the wood itself and the ground around it. Finally, grinning at my discovery, I retrieved my dry wood and carried it to the fire pit in the campsite next to us.

*　　*　　*

An hour later I sat by the fire, my feet propped on a log, a cup of coffee in my hand. Overhead an orange-yellow sunrise chased the gray from the sky, promising another beautiful day. I heard Sue walking toward me before I saw her.

"Good morning," she chirped as she stood beside me, holding her hands to the warmth of the fire. "It's going to be another nice day."

"Yes, it is."

"So we go on down the lake today?"

"Yes, we do."

"Good. I feel rested and strong. I need a good day of paddling."

I waited. When she said nothing more, I finally blurted out, "Aren't you going to ask me?"

"Ask you what?" Sue answered with an innocent look.

"Ask me why I built our fire in *this* campsite instead of our own campsite."

"No, I don't think so," she replied, shaking her head.

"Why not?"

"Because I try never to interrupt you when you're doing something weird."

"Now I'm not *going* to tell you."

"Yes, you are," Sue grinned. "You're dying to tell me."

"I built it here because I didn't want to destroy the evidence in our own campsite before you got a chance to see it."

"What evidence?"

"Evidence that solves the puzzle of last night's eating sounds."

"Wait a minute," Sue protested, dropping her playful mood. "You're going to show me something horrible, aren't you? A half-eaten deer or something."

"No, actually I'm going to show you something you'll probably like."

"Not something horrible and bloody?"

"No. The thing that woke us up last night was something *you'd* call cute and cuddly."

"Cute and cudd . . . ? Oh, my porcupine?"

"Right. Your porcupine. Come with me."

*   *   *

"My trophy guy made this mess?" Sue asked as we neared our fire pit.

"Uh huh. It turns out your porcupine has a taste for charcoal. Look at this." I picked up a thick branch that had been dragged from the fire. "See how both ends are scorched and charcoaled, but the middle section isn't? See these chew marks? Your buddy held this branch down with its front feet and chewed the middle. Look here," I pointed. "Another chomped-up piece. They're scattered all over the place."

"So how do you know it was my porcupine?" Sue asked. "Maybe it was a beaver or something. They chew wood, don't they?"

"Come here," I beckoned as I knelt by the muddy area near the pit. "See these tracks? Porcupine tracks. Four toes on the front foot. Five toes on the back. These prints that look like a human baby's foot are the back feet of a porcupine."

"Human baby?" Sue objected. "Look at the size of those toenails. Maybe Rosemary's baby but not a human baby."

"Well, you know what I mean," I laughed. "Other animals leave prints with that shape, too—raccoons, muskrats, some others. But here's the final proof this was your boy. See these marks between the footprints? The ones that look as if someone dragged a straw broom along here? The quills on his tail make those. Nope, no getting around it. Your trophy boyfriend spent the night dining here."

"You're probably right about the porcupine's being my boyfriend," Sue smiled, hooking her arm through mine as we returned to our fire. "I think I do attract porcupine-like characters."

"No doubt about it," I answered. "You're definitely a porcupine-magnet kind of girl."

*   *   *

We had finished loading the canoe, and I was tying in the last of the gear when Sue reminded me, "Don't forget we promised to stop by Larry and Stan's camp if we left before they did."

"Right," I answered. Then I jerked upright. "Wait a minute! Wait just a minute! I can't believe I missed that!"

"What?" Sue asked, startled.

"They *knew*! Those guys *knew*!"

"What do you mean they knew? Knew what?"

"They knew about the porcupine. All that stuff about did we have a good night's sleep. Their Abbott-and-Costello routine about sleep sometimes being disturbed up here. And how the storm probably kept everything hunkered down the night before. Remember all that?"

"You're right," Sue laughed. "They knew."

SUE'S PORCUPINE COLLECTION

Paddling wide around the mouth of Turner Creek, we angled toward the campground on the other side. Four canoes lay overturned on the bank.

We made our way past two campsites of canoeists, one packing up and the other leisurely enjoying a late breakfast. As we walked up the path to the shelter, we saw Stan sitting on the steps, coffee cup in hand. He turned and said something into the interior of the opened door. In response Larry emerged from the shelter, wiping a tin plate with a towel.

"You knew!" I shouted as we drew near.

"What?" Stan asked, an innocent look not quite disguising the beginning of a grin.

"Don't give me that," I challenged as we reached the bottom step. "You knew."

"Knew what?"

"Knew about the porcupine!"

"Porcupine? What porcupine?" But they couldn't hold back. Laughing, Stan rolled backward on the porch, spilling his coffee, and Larry, slapping the towel against his leg, doubled over, roaring.

"He's a beauty, isn't he?" Larry laughed, tears running down his cheeks. "Biggest darn porkie I ever saw."

"Come on up here," Stan said. "Coffee's hot, and Larry made some camp biscuits in case you want something different from instant oatmeal."

*　　*　　*

"We've stayed on that side of the creek the last two years," Stan explained as we sat on the porch with our coffee and honey-drizzled biscuits, "and that porcupine was there both times. The first year we figured it was just passing through, but last year we realized it lived there."

"And chewing charcoal all night long is his thing," Larry grinned.

"So, why didn't you tell us?" I demanded.

"What good would that have done?" Stan replied. "You were all settled in. Wouldn't have packed up and moved, would you?"

"No, but maybe we would have slept easier knowing it was a porcupine and not Big Foot eating his way through our campground."

"You're right," Stan agreed, grinning. "That was bad of us."

"On the other hand," Larry offered, "part of the fun up here is running into the unexpected."

"What do you think, Sue?" Stan asked, turning to her. "Is part of the fun up here running into the unexpected?"

"Yes, I think it is," Sue smiled. "And the most unexpected thing I've encountered so far this morning is these scrumptious biscuits Larry made."

"Then maybe you'd better have another," Larry gushed, flattered by Sue's praise, a schoolboy blush spreading over the cheeks above his grizzled beard.

Well, I smiled to myself, *Sue seems to have added another porcupine to her collection.*

GOING WITH THE FLOW

Stan and Larry accompanied us to the lake, where they stood at the water's edge, watching me steady the canoe while Sue made her way into the bow. "How far you going today?" Stan asked, shading his eyes from the sun already hot in a cloudless sky.

"Unna," I answered. "How about you two?"

"Unna," Stan replied.

"Okay then." I stepped into the stern of the canoe and pushed off. "See you down there."

*   *   *

We had paddled five minutes before Sue asked over her shoulder, "So, what's Unna?"

"Unna is quite possibly my favorite lake on the circuit. It's a pristine gem. You'll love it."

"Okay," she answered nonchalantly, turning back and leaning into her stroke.

"And from the lake there's a trail, a mile or so to Cariboo Falls. They're magnificent."

"Okay," she repeated.

"But between here and there, we have two more stretches of the Cariboo River. The first is slow water, but it's still murky and has some deadheads and sweepers. So you'll have to be our eyes again."

"No problem," she said, without turning around.

No problem, I thought to myself, smiling at this new confidence—almost cockiness—in Sue. *Okay* to my choice of tonight's camp and *okay* to a mile-long hike to see a waterfalls. Those casual responses I might have expected. But *no problem* to another stretch of murky river with deadheads and sweepers?

"You're certainly casual about all this," I said. "And that's good because this stretch isn't anywhere near the challenge of the upper river. I'm impressed with this new attitude. In fact, I'm tempted to say you're so relaxed you're just going with the flow."

To her silence, I repeated, "Just going with the flow. Get it? We're canoeing down a lake and you're going with the flow?"

"I get it. I get it," Sue threw back. "But I can't believe you're saying something so corny."

"Corny? I don't think it's corny. In fact, if I ever write about this trip, that'll be my title. *Going with the Flow.*"

"Well, if you want anyone to read it, you'd better come up with a better title."

"No, I like it. *Going with the Flow.* A perfect title for a canoeing adventure."

"It's corny," Sue declared with a stamp of finality.

*   *   *

The current doesn't change much at the point where Lanezi Lake drains into the Cariboo River. The shorelines narrow, and the water shallows, but the surface remains a slow, cloudy drift of glacial water.

"This is so easy," Sue announced twenty minutes into our paddle down the river.

"Well, don't get too relaxed," I answered. "You still need to be on the lookout for deadheads and sweepers."

"I know," Sue said. "I was just commenting on how eas . . . Wait! Look up there!"

I backstroked to slow the canoe and looked over her shoulder, expecting to see a deadhead or some other hazard. But Sue was pointing to the shoreline.

On the left bank ahead of us, a large black bear strolled along the rocky shore, stopping occasionally to turn over stones and nose the ground. With its rump to us, it moved in a comic waddle along the water's edge.

We pulled to the middle of the river and lifted our paddles, letting the current carry us downstream toward the bear.

"What's he doing?" Sue asked.

"My guess is there's something in the rocks he likes to eat."

"Do you think he knows we're here?"

"Maybe not yet. But he'll probably hear or smell us before he sees us."

As if on cue, the bear leaned back on its haunches, pointed its nose upward, and began swinging its head from side to side, testing the air. Following the scent to us, it turned and stared in our direction. Finally focusing, it watched our approach down the river.

"Are we okay?" Sue asked.

"We're fine," I reassured her.

Dismissing us, the bear dropped to all fours and continued its search along the rocky shore. We drifted by, completely ignored.

"Well," Sue said, "he was far less interested in us than we were in him."

"You're right," I agreed. "That was one laid-back bear. In fact, it was so laid-back, I'd say that was a bear just going with the flow."

In answer, Sue swept a shallow stroke across the surface of the river, throwing a spray of water into my face and chest.

"Hey!" I yelled.

She giggled and swept another spray into me. In defense, I retaliated with my own sweeping stroke forward, soaking her from the neck downward.

"Truce!" Sue laughed. "Truce!"

"Truce," I agreed.

Our water fight over, we brought the rocking canoe under control and continued on our way down the Cariboo River.

Going with the flow.

A CREEK BY ANY OTHER NAME . . .

"Do you think one of those is Stan and Larry?" Sue asked as we watched four canoes moving down Sandy Lake toward the beach where we had stopped for lunch.

"I doubt it," I answered, sorting through a handful of gorp to discard the walnut bits.

"I don't understand why you don't like walnuts," Sue remarked.

"Really? *I* don't understand why squirrels *do*. Still, they can have all these."

"So why don't you think Stan and Larry are in one of those canoes?"

"Because that looks like a single group traveling together. Stan and Larry don't strike me as the type to hook up with others."

"Me either," Sue agreed. "But while you've been so painstaking picking through your lunch, I've been watching those canoes. See that one on the right, the green one? Isn't that the color of Stan and Larry's canoe?"

"Uh huh," I answered, "along with about half the other canoes on the circuit."

"Yes, but if you look closely, you'll note the green canoe is passing the others. I think that canoe's trying to get ahead for the run down the lake."

"You know what, Eagle Eye? I believe you're right. And trying to beat the others down the lake is *exactly* what Stan and Larry would do."

"It is, isn't it?" Sue grinned.

"In any case, we'd better pack up and get out on the lake ahead of them," I said, rising to my feet and turning to offer Sue a hand.

"Why?" Sue frowned, ignoring my hand and squirming into a more comfortable position in the sand. "I like it here. This is such a pretty lake. What's the rush?"

"First of all, I'm a little concerned about those thunderheads," I replied, looking upward. In the past thirty minutes, dark-edged clouds had rolled over the ridge behind us.

"Second, there's only one campground on Unna Lake. We don't know how many people are already there, and here come four more canoes. We need to beat them to the lake."

"Oh, all right," Sue grumbled, "but we'll look pretty silly rushing around to pack our stuff and shoving off right in front of them. I mean, how obvious is that?"

"They're still at least half a mile up the lake. If we get moving now, we'll hardly be shoving off right in front of them."

Sue reluctantly started rise but then pushed back down. "Wait a minute. You haven't told me what to expect on the next stretch of river. You always prepare me for our next adventure." She lay back, cupping her hands behind her head. "So prepare me. I'm listening."

"The next stretch of river is just like the last one," I sighed. "A bit wider, maybe, that's all. You'll still have to watch out for deadheads, and the current is a little stronger but not really enough to notice."

"How do you know it's stronger if it isn't strong enough to notice?"

"Well, you won't notice it going down the river, but you'll feel it when we come back."

"Come back?" Sue asked, sitting up. "What do you mean, come back? We're going to turn around and come back up the river?"

"Unna's a little bit of a detour," I began. "There's a big bend in the river that actually goes around the lake instead of through it the way the river does with Lanezi and Sandy. That's one of the reasons Unna's so refreshing. Finally a clear mountain lake not full of silt from the river."

"But why is it a detour?"

"We're on the south side of the circuit," I explained. "A small creek connects the south side with the west side. And we have to travel up that creek to the last series of lakes on the circuit. But the creek empties into the Cariboo River about halfway into the bend around Unna Lake, and the entrance to the lake is at the far end of the bend, approximately a quarter of a mile on down the river. So visiting Unna involves a detour. But it's a detour well worth the extra effort."

Seeing the glazed look in Sue's eyes, I asked, "Do you want me to go over that again?"

"No. I may have been a little distracted by the bends in the river and the south side versus the west or whatever, but I got the gist of it. Basically, we go by the place where we're supposed to go up a creek as part of the regular circuit so that we can go on down to Unna Lake, and tomorrow we have to paddle back up the river a quarter of a mile to return to the creek."

"See," I grinned. "I do explain things clearly."

"No," Sue replied, shaking her head. "Women have a built-in radar we can plug in when men begin explaining things in a technically tedious fashion. This radar helps us sift through your explanations, discarding the chaff from the essential, just as you discard walnut bits from gorp."

Suddenly Sue began to giggle. "It's not that funny," I groused. "All that bit about feminine radar. Not that funny."

"Oh, no, not that. It's just that I realized tomorrow we'll paddle up a creek and . . ." She collapsed into more laughter.

"And what? What's so hilarious?"

"Doesn't that strike you as funny?" Sue giggled. "People always talk about being up a creek without a paddle, but we're actually going to paddle up a creek."

"Well, you're probably not going to paddle much of it. Three Mile Creek is pretty shallow. We'll line most of it."

"Tell me again what you mean when you say we'll line something."

"It's one of the neatest things about canoes. You can wade up a shallow creek, pulling the canoe behind, and it'll follow just like a well-trained dog. It's really a cool thing to do."

"We're going to pull the canoe up a creek for three miles?"

"No, not three miles. More like three quarters of a mile."

"Oh, I see," Sue replied. "We don't go up the entire creek. We leave it somewhere along the way."

"No, we follow the entire creek. It drains from the first lake we paddle on the west side."

"But you said it's called Three Mile Creek. Why is it called Three Mile Creek if it isn't three miles long?"

"I don't know."

"Well, guess."

"I guess it's called Three Mile Creek because Three Quarters of a Mile Creek would be awkward."

"Admit it," Sue demanded. "It doesn't make sense to call a creek Three Mile Creek when it isn't even long enough to be called One Mile Creek."

"Okay, I'll admit you have a point, and I suppose I have to tell you something. I call it Three Mile Creek because that was its name the first time I canoed the circuit. I still have the map that lists it as Three Mile

Creek. But on later maps, including the one we're using now, it's called Babcock Creek. There. Does that make you feel better?"

"Yes, it does," Sue grinned. "And I might add, 'Good for him.'"

"Good for him? What him?"

"Good for Babcock. Obviously someone named Babcock realized how silly the name was. I assume when he pointed this out to the powers that be, they named the creek after him."

"Actually it's called that because it runs out of Babcock Lake."

"Wow! They must have really been impressed to name the lake after him, too."

In frustration I turned aside just in time to see the green canoe bearing down on us, Stan and Larry grinning as they pulled near.

"Hey, you two," Stan called. "Did you change your mind about going to Unna today?"

"No," I answered. "We'll be there."

"Well, if you want some advice, I'd suggest you get underway. Looks like some weather rolling in. Could pin everybody down at Unna, and there's only one campground on the lake. That's a bunch of Boy Scouts coming behind us," Stan added, thumbing over his shoulder. "Be a good idea to beat them down there."

"Thanks," I answered as they glided by. "Never would have thought of that."

"Are you ready now?" I asked, turning to Sue. "Or do you want to hold us up until the Scouts go by?"

"What? You're blaming me for this delay? I'm not the one who changed the subject."

"What are you talking about?" I asked, kneeling to pick up our day pack.

"All I did was pose a simple question about the river, and you went off on a tangent about a creek with a silly name. I was ready to go before all that, but I love it when you go into your teacher mode."

"Thank you," I replied.

"You're welcome." Sue smiled.

*   *   *

We had just entered the Cariboo River, leaving Sandy Lake behind, when Sue asked over her shoulder, "So this entire river goes over a giant waterfall somewhere ahead of us?"

"Yes, but don't worry. There are signs warning canoeists against going beyond a certain point."

"Of course," Sue replied. "No doubt put there by Babcock himself."

"No doubt about it, Babes," I agreed. "No doubt at all."

THE PARIS HILTON

"**This is really beautiful,**" Sue said as we lifted our paddles, allowing the canoe to drift into Unna Lake. A shaft of sunlight had broken through the black clouds overhead. Green-blue water mirrored lodgepole pines on the slopes circling the lake. From the pines to the sandy beaches stretched a carpet of moss, a patchwork of emerald and light yellow-green.

"It's so beautiful," Sue repeated, turning to look at me. "Can we stay here an extra day?"

"If we can *find* a place to stay," I answered. The beach below the campground was crowded with canoes. Dodging the canoes, a number of young people ran in and out of the water, shrieking from the shock of the cold mountain lake.

"It does look crowded, doesn't it?" Sue replied, "but we have to find a place here. We just *have* to." Beneath the excitement in her voice was a special urgency. We hadn't been in a crowd since leaving Isaac Lake two days before. Sue saw an opportunity here.

"What about down there?" she asked, pointing to the south shore of the lake. "There aren't as many canoes. Maybe we'll have a better chance of finding a campsite there."

"That's not a campground, Babes."

"Yes, it is," she argued. "I can see packs in a bear cache. Don't you see that?"

"Yes, that's a bear cache, but there's no campground. That's the starting point of the trail to Cariboo Falls. People put their packs in the cache before they hike the trail."

Sue thought a moment before observing, "If those people don't have their packs in the campgrounds here, they must not be staying on the lake tonight. Maybe some of these other people are just using the campgrounds for a break before going on. There might be more room than you think."

177

"Perhaps we should ask Stan and Larry," I suggested.

"That's a good idea," Sue replied. "They might even have saved us a spot. Let's go look for them."

"We don't have to look far. They're standing on the beach, waving at us right now."

*　　*　　*

"You made good time," Larry said, steadying the canoe so that Sue could step from the bow. "We've been here only a half hour ourselves."

"Did you get a campsite?" Sue asked.

"Yes, but I'm afraid it was the last one. We thought about trying to find two together to save one for you, but we were lucky to nab the one we did."

"Don't worry, Babes," I comforted her as Larry and I pulled the canoe onto the beach. "We're going to stay here even if we have to resort to an unauthorized campsite. It's too late to return to Three Mile Cre . . . I mean Babcock Creek."

"But what about those people hiking to the falls?" Sue asked. "Isn't it too late for them, too?"

"Probably. I suspect we'll see a number of unauthorized campsites before the day is through especially if these clouds open up. Let's start scouting for a place we can use."

"Bob," Stan said in a lowered voice as he stepped nearer, "I have two words for you." He leaned forward and whispered, "Rum Lake."

"Rum Lake? It has a campground?" He nodded a silent yes.

"This is my sixth trip on the circuit, but I've never gone into Rum Lake. It has a campground, huh?"

"Shh. Not so loud," he whispered, holding a finger to his lips. No one in the campground behind us could have heard our conversation, but Stan was clearly enjoying his cloak-and-dagger moment.

"Do we have to go to another lake?" Sue asked in a normal voice that brought another hushing from Stan. "I don't want to. I want to stay here."

"It's okay, Babes," I smiled, putting an arm around her shoulder. "In fact, it might be better than okay. It might be perfect."

She shook her head, obviously disappointed, not only by the possible loss of Unna Lake but also the loss of the crowd."

"It's right next door," I whispered, continuing Stan's game. "There's a little inlet from this lake to that one. It's a tiny little thing hidden on the other side of that rise over there." I nodded to the north shore. "Unless they study the map, most people wouldn't even know another lake's there."

"But that means we'll be the only ones in the campground," she pouted.

"There's a trail around both lakes," Stan offered. "It connects the two campgrounds. A ten-minute walk will bring you right back here. You can visit all you like, and, anyway, when people realize you've found a place over there, you could be flooded with company."

"But if we don't get going," I interjected, "we might still lose out."

"Then what are we waiting for?" Sue demanded. "Let's do it."

*   *   *

"Oh, this is so cute," Sue purred, as we paddled toward the campground on the other side of Rum Lake.

"Yes, it is," I agreed. "Same beaches, same pines as Unna, but everything in miniature."

"It's baby version of Unna Lake," Sue laughed. "I love it."

She quit paddling and leaned over the left gunnel to trail her hand in the ripples from the canoe's bow. "And the water's so much warmer."

"Uh huh," I answered. "Water is usually warmer in shallow lakes."

"It feels so good. Warm water. It feels so . . . Oh," she gasped, jerking her hand from the water and picking up her paddle with a special urgency, "we have to hurry. I really need to go to the bathroom."

*   *   *

I had our ground tarp spread and was positioning our tent when Sue returned from her rushed trip up the trail to the campground's pit toilet. "This is a *great* camp," she bubbled. "Wait till you see the outhouse."

"Really," I smiled, laying out the tent poles.

"It's amazing," Sue continued. "It's up on that hill behind us. And wait till you see the view! The open side—you know, the side that doesn't have a wall—it looks out over the lake. You have this perfectly beautiful view when you're in there. Not only that. It's really clean as if someone just tidied it up. And, are you ready for this? It has toilet paper! *Two rolls*! That's the first time I've seen toilet paper on the whole trip."

When I chuckled, her face clouded over. "What's so funny?"

"Nothing," I answered. "It's just that I haven't seen you so excited for a while. And to think the cause of this exuberance is an outhouse."

"Well, some things are more important than others," Sue smiled. "This outhouse isn't just nice. It's *super* nice. It's the Paris Hilton of all outhouses."

"Okay," I replied, kneeling to drive in a tent peg. "As soon as we have camp set up, I'll go have a look for myself."

"I'll go with you," Sue enthused. "I want to see your reaction."

"Normally, that's a trip I prefer to take by myself," I grinned. "But the Paris Hilton of all outhouses? I guess that's an experience we need to share."

"Oh, go ahead. Make fun of me. But this is really the best outhouse I've ever seen."

"You know what?" I said a few minutes later, having fastened the tent fly into place. "When we get home, I'm going to take you on a field trip up the Clackamas River. I helped build a couple of its campgrounds when I worked for the Forest Service. And most of them have really nice outhouses. Toilet paper and everything. You'll love them."

"You promise?" Sue laughed.

"Cross my heart," I answered, making the appropriate gesture. "Now help me set up the rest of the camp. The rain isn't going to hold back much longer."

"Okay, but you don't get to go to the Paris Hilton without me."

"Babes," I answered, releasing a sleeping bag from one of the pack frames, "I promised—and I'll keep my promise—the first time I visit the outhouse, you can go with me."

"Oh," she grinned, taking the sleeping bag from me, "you're so good to me."

RAIN AND OLD SAYINGS

The rain began just as I positioned the first of our two backpacks onto the bear cache. The drops were gentle at first, like tiny fingers lightly tapping my shoulders and upper back as I reached for a dangling bungee cord that I had looped over the pack. But before I could catch the cord as it swayed in a breeze quickly becoming a wind, the fingers became more insistent, and I knew I was in for a soaking before I could get the second pack into place.

From the shelter of a pine, Sue called up to me. "It's starting to rain. I'm heading back to the tent. See you there." When I turned to look down, she was already gone. Grumbling, I started down the ladder for the other pack.

Fifteen minutes later, I crawled into the tent. Sue, sitting Indian style, held a towel in her lap. After I had pulled off my muddy boots, I began unbuttoning my shirt.

"You're soaked," she observed, tossing the towel to me.

"Really?" I muttered, pulling off the shirt.

"Really," she affirmed.

"Well, maybe I wouldn't be so wet if you had stuck around to help."

"Oh, right," Sue answered. "Let's see. You at the top of the ladder, rain-slicked backpack in hand, and me standing below, innocently trying to help. You know what? Been there. Done that. Not exactly a set of conditions conducive to my well-being."

"I guess not," I agreed, sheepishly.

"Nope," Sue said, shaking her head. "What's that old saying? 'Drop a pack on my head once, shame on you. Drop a pack on my head twice, shame on me.'"

"That's a little bit of an improvisation, but I guess it's appropriate," I smiled.

"And speaking of that little misadventure of mine," Sue replied, sweeping off her hat and tilting her head forward, "how do I look?"

I studied the butterflies still in place. A half-moon of quarter-inch hair had filled in the shaved area. "Perfect," I answered. "Can't even see it anymore."

"Really?"

"No, not really. But it looks better than it did a few days ago. By the time we get home, you'll be able to disguise it with an old man's comb-over."

"Oh, good," she laughed. "Well, you know what they say. 'A stitch in time saves nine.'"

"Hand me my sweatshirt, will you?" I asked, motioning to the rolled shirt and jacket I used for a pillow each night. "And do me a favor. Enough of the tired old sayings."

"Okay," Sue answered, tossing the sweatshirt to me. "So now what? I'm going to take a little nap. How about you?"

"No, I think I'll read for a while."

"Oh, too bad," she replied, lying back and then turning to her side and curling into her favorite sleeping position.

"Why too bad?" I asked, reaching for my book.

"It's just that I wanted to say, 'Nighty night. Sleep tight. Don't let the bedbugs . . .' Ouch. That hurt," she objected, rubbing her shoulder where I had swatted her with the book.

"Go to sleep," I pleaded. "Please."

"All right," Sue smiled. She scooted up, kissed me lightly on the cheek, and then returned to her curled position. In a few minutes, her breathing slowed and deepened. She was fast asleep.

*　　*　　*

I awoke to voices in the campground outside our tent. I lay on my back, my book on my chest, where it must have dropped when I fell asleep. At my side, Sue was sitting up, grinning. "Someone's here," she whispered.

"Yes," I answered. "I hear them."

"I'm going out to see who they are," she announced, moving forward toward the tent's opening.

"Maybe you should give them time to set up a camp," I suggested, my hand on her shoulder.

"Oh, I guess," she answered, disappointed. "But anyway," she brightened, "we'll have company tonight."

"Did the rain stop?" I asked.

"Uh huh. About a half hour ago. You were really out of it."

I crawled to the tent's opening and pulled back the flap. A glimmering ray of sunlight moved across the lake as the sky cleared. "We might have a good night," I remarked. "And hopefully a good day tomorrow to hike to the falls."

"Well, I always say, 'You reap what you sow.'"

"What does *that* mean?"

"I don't know," Sue grinned. "I'm running out of sayings."

"Thank God," I laughed. "I guess it's true. 'Good things come to him who waits.'"

"Okay," she smiled. "You win. No more old sayings."

"Really?"

"Really. You win. 'To the victor go the spoils.'"

"I have an idea," I replied. "Why don't you go check out the new arrivals?"

"You think I should? You think they've had enough time to set up their camp?"

"Go ahead," I smiled. "They might as well find out what they're in for right away." I'd hardly finished the sentence before she disappeared out the front of the tent.

Picking up my book, I lay back and begin thumbing through the pages. "Now let's see. Where was I?"

*   *   *

Forty minutes later, Sue returned with a flourish. Tossing back the tent flap, she threw herself onto her sleeping bag. I looked over my book at her. She was bubbling with excitement. "It's beautiful out there. Let's go out and hike that trail around the lakes."

"Okay, just let me finish this chapter, and then we'll go."

"Oh, all right. But hurry."

I read to the bottom of the page, all too aware of her stare, her impatient drumming of fingers on her leg. I turned the page. She sighed. I looked up.

"Don't you want to know who's out there?" she demanded.

I lay the book aside. "All right. Who's out there?"

"Scouts. Not *my* scouts, the ones who helped with my head. These are the ones we saw coming down Sandy Lake. They're from Lynden,

Washington. It's a town right near the U.S.-Canadian border. I told them they're so lucky to live where they do because they can come to Canada any time they want. Well, that wasn't exactly the thing to say because no one wants to think his hometown is just where you go to get to somewhere else, so they started to tell me all about how living in Lynden was so great, especially for outdoors types like themselves because of all the fishing and everything. It's so cute how proud they are of their town. They had all kinds of reasons we should go through there on our way home. They're a nice bunch of kids. There's one you'll *really* like. His name is Jimmy. He's a real cutie. And get this. He's a Blazer fan! That's right! A Blazer fan from northern Washington. But it figures because he's really from Portland. His dad got a job in Lynden last year, and they had to move. He takes a lot of kidding from the other scouts because they're Sonics fans, of course. But he handles it well. In fact, he rubs it in because he's the only one who's really gone to an NBA game. All the others have seen games on TV but not in person. Jimmy and his dad went to Blazer games at least two or three times a year when they lived in Portland. And get this. Jimmy lived in the Mount Tabor neighborhood. Right where I grew up. We talked about parks and stores that I used to go to when I was a teenager, and they're still there. Jimmy went to the same places. I think he got a little homesick when we talked. Anyway, you're going to like these kids. And the scoutmaster seems like a nice guy, too."

She stopped to take a breath. Then seeing my expression, she started to giggle. When I didn't say anything, she stopped giggling but, still smiling, concluded, "I guess that about covers it."

"Well, if you're through, let's go for that hike."

"Are you sure? I thought you wanted to finish a chapter."

"No, I'm not in the mood to read."

"I could tell you didn't really want to read. After all, you've barely read a single page since I came back."

*   *   *

As we walked away from our camp, I asked, "So should I have you on a leash?"

"What? What are you talking about?"

"It's just that when you get like this, you're like a cocker spaniel on speed. I keep expecting you to dart off into the brush and get lost or something."

"Oh, don't worry about that," Sue grinned, taking my hand and leaning into me. "I won't dart off. You know why?"

"Why?"

"Because it's what they always say. 'A cocker spaniel in the hand is worth two in the bush.'"

Laughing and bumping shoulders like a pair of flirtatious teenagers, we set off on our hike around the lakes.

MARSHMALLOWS AND CAMPFIRE STORIES

Because we had taken the long way around Unna on our afternoon hike, the sun was already dipping behind the western ridges by the time Sue and I reached the lake's campground. "We can stay only a few minutes," I instructed as we looked for Stan and Larry's campsite.

"But the whole purpose of the hike was to visit," Sue pouted. "And Stan said the trail between here and our campground on Rum Lake is only a ten-minute walk."

"That's true, but do you really want to hike it in the dark?"

"Hike what in the dark?" Stan asked, coming toward us with an armload of firewood. All around us, the crowded campground was coming to life with evening fires.

"Oh, Bob says we can't stay even though we just got here. He's afraid of the dark."

"Don't blame him. A bear in the day is unpleasant. Walk up on one in the dark, and you're in for a long night."

"They sleep at night just like us," Sue sniffed. "Why would they be out wandering around?"

"I don't know. But is that something you really want to chance?"

"Oh, I know," Sue sighed. "You're both right, of course. It's just that I was really looking forward to some socializing. A nice evening with friends around the fire. I know you guys like this macho one-on-one with nature and all that. But I enjoy company, that's all."

"I'll tell you what," Stan said. "How about Larry and I come by your camp after dinner."

"Oh, right," Sue replied. "It's too dangerous for *us* to hike in the . . . what would you call this?" she asked, holding up her hands and looking to the sky. "Early dusk? But you and Larry can hike the trail after the real dark sets in?"

"No, we won't walk. We'll canoe over."

"Oh, sure. Canoe in the dark."

"Right. Night paddling is fun. You'd be surprised how much more light there is on the water. The only problem is near shore. Harder to see there. So the inlet into Rum Lake could be a little tricky, but we have flashlights."

"How're you going to paddle and hold flashlights at the same time?"

"We won't. These are headlamps like the kind coal miners use. They free up your hands."

"Now that's a clever idea," Sue said, warming to the possibility of evening guests. "And you'll come? Really?"

"We'll be there," Stan smiled.

"Come on, Bob," Sue said, taking my hand and pulling me forward. "We're going to have company tonight. I have some planning to do."

*　　*　　*

I watched Sue across the fire. Hands up, palms outward, she rocked from side to side as she pantomimed her sand-spit bear. Her audience—five wide-eyed Boy Scouts, a scoutmaster who looked young enough to be one of his charges, and Gus and Marge, a pair of Floridians who had arrived at the campground while Sue and I were on our hike—all leaned forward, caught up in her narrative. Stan and Larry, sitting by me, seemed to enjoy her story as much this time as they had the first time they heard it.

"She's really got it down pat," Stan whispered, leaning toward me. "It's a great bear story."

I nodded, not taking my eyes off her as she continued her tale. Sue was in her element. Not because she was the center of attention but because she had people enjoying themselves in the company of others. And I realized, not for the first time, why people are so attracted to her. Sue has a genuine interest in every person she meets. No matter the age—three or eight-three—everyone feels special with Sue.

"Who wants another marshmallow?" she asked, having concluded her story. She picked up the package and passed it to Marvin, the youngest scout, who had instinctively moved closer to her throughout the evening. "Don't be shy. I've carried them all this way just for an evening like this.

And, by the way, we owe special thanks to Jimmy and Alan. They cut these roasting sticks for us."

"I wish *we'd* see a bear," Jimmy complained, poking a pair of marshmallows onto his stick. "We've come all this way and haven't seen a single bear."

"We haven't either," Marge offered. "But I can't say I'm not glad."

"Do you have bears in Florida?" Jimmy asked.

"Now that's a good question," Gus smiled. "Contrary to what most folks on this side of the continent might believe, we do have bears. The Florida black bear. There aren't as many as the black bears up here, of course, but we do have bears. What we really have a lot of, however, is alligators."

"I know!" one of the scouts blurted. "My family went to Orlando last year, and everyone there talked about alligators. They come up into people's yards and everything. Have you ever had one in your yard?"

"No," Gus shook his head, "but I've seen them on the golf course."

"Whoa!" Stan exclaimed. "Now that's what I'd call a real hazard. How do you handle an alligator on a golf course?"

"Oh, no problem," Gus grinned. "You just let him play through."

"I think I was just set up," Stan shouted over the laughter.

"That's one of Gus's more tired old jokes," Marge sympathized. "Don't get him started."

"It's a Florida joke," Gus laughed. "We have to save it for trips out of state."

"Well, when you two make a trip out of state, you sure make a long one," Gary, the scoutmaster, observed. "All the way from Florida to British Columbia, now that's some trip."

"I know," Marge smiled. "We thought we should get some kind of prize. You know, like those you get at reunions for the people who've traveled the farthest to get there. But then we started running into all these Europeans on the circuit."

"Speaking of Europeans," Larry began, offering his first words of the evening, "have you run into that couple from Switzerland? What're their names, Sue?"

"Albin and Christina."

"Yeah. Albin and Christina. Anyone run across them? No? Well, anyway, this Albin tells a great story about being pinned under his rig in the Sahara Desert while a scorpion runs around on him."

"*The Beast*," Stan interjected.

"Right," Larry nodded. "*The Beast*. That's what they call their rig. Some kind of modified army vehicle. Anyway, there he was, trapped under *The Beast* with that big scorpion crawling all over him."

"What happened?" one of the scouts breathed.

"Oh, he managed to escape without being stung, but it's quite a story."

Marge shook her head. "The Sahara Desert. I can't imagine traveling in such place. No sane person would do that."

"You think not?" Sue grinned. "It just so happens Bob has a story about being lost in the Sahara Desert."

"Really?" someone gasped, and suddenly all eyes were on me.

"I wasn't lost," I said, shrugging. "I was stranded. And it was barely out into the desert. Just a couple of miles or so. Mostly I spent a day trying to find a way out of the Nile Valley."

"Tell us," Gus commanded. "That has to be a great story."

"Oh, it's far too long to tell tonight," I said, shaking my head.

"Come on, Bob," Sue encouraged. "Give us an abridged edition."

"Come on," someone across the fire seconded.

"Well, okay, I guess. The way it happened was a friend and I started out on a trip to Kenya. Unfortunately, we didn't get there. Instead, we got stonewalled in Cairo when some bureaucrats figured out we'd bought our tickets with black-market rupees."

"What's a rupee?" Martin asked.

"That's what people in Pakistan call their money. I was living in Pakistan at the time."

"Where's Pakistan?"

"Martin," Gary admonished, "Bob is never going to tell us the story if you keep interrupting him with questions."

"It's okay," I said, seeing, even in the hazy light of the smoky campfire, Martin's embarrassment. "You know where India is?"

"Yeah," Martin replied, breaking into a wide smile. "We studied the Taj Mahal last year."

"Okay, then. Pakistan is right next to India. And don't be embarrassed about not knowing where Pakistan is. A lot of *adults* don't know where it is. In fact, when I was offered a job there, I had to look it up myself."

"So how'd you get lost in the Sahara Desert?" Jimmy asked impatiently.

"My friend and I decided that since we were stuck in Cairo a few extra days, we'd travel out to a set of pyramids that are much older than those you usually see in the pictures. So we asked someone how to get there . . .

*   *   *

" . . . and that's how we finally got back to Cairo," I finished twenty minutes later.

"Did you get to see the James Bond movie?" Alan asked.

"Yeah, we did. Fortunately they have midnight showings in Cairo."

"And speaking of midnight," Stan yawned, rising to his feet, "Larry and I need to call it a night." As if on cue, all the others began to rise and stretch.

"Bob, can I ask you a question?" Marge inquired. "Something's been bothering me all night."

"Sure, I guess."

"I've been watching you. You haven't eaten a single marshmallow. You didn't even take a roasting stick. So what's the story? Were you just saving them for guests, or do you have something against marshmallows?"

"Oh," Sue laughed, "Bob doesn't eat sweets. I used to bake wedding cakes. He'd help me take them to receptions and set them up, but I don't think he ever ate a piece."

"Seriously?" Marge asked. "How can someone not eat wedding cake?"

"Gets me," Sue smiled. "But I'll bet if you dipped a marshmallow in Scotch, he'd eat it."

"I would," I agreed, "but that would be a terrible thing to do to Scotch."

"Oh, by the way, Bob," Stan said, slipping on his jacket, "be sure you burn all these roasting sticks and do a good job cleaning up around the fire. Nothing like a little melted marshmallow to bring in the night visitors."

"Bears?" Jimmy asked, excited by the prospect.

"Maybe," Stan replied, "or perhaps something else. Maybe even a porcupine." He nudged Larry, who erupted into laughter.

"What's this about porcupines?" Gus asked.

"Never mind," I answered. "It's a long story."

"But it's a good one," Stan threw back over his shoulder as Larry and he started down the trail to the lake. "It's a good one."

*   *   *

Sue and I stood on the water's edge watching the lights of Stan and Larry's headlamps bob and sway as they crossed Rum Lake. Finally, the lights winked out as the canoe entered the inlet from Unna and disappeared into the darkness.

"This was a perfect evening," Sue said softly, moving closer into the protective embrace of my arm around her waist. "I'm ready to take on the rest of the circuit now."

"Good. But not tomorrow. Tomorrow we hike to the falls. Other than that, we have the day to just laze around. And judging from these stars," I added, looking overhead, "a beautiful day it's going to be."

DAY 9

MUSINGS AT A WATERFALL

We heard Cariboo Falls long before we arrived. The roar of an angry river plunging over a cliff into a canyon eighty feet below.

The trail had been an easy walk, less than a mile through an open forest of tall, skinny lodgepole pines in a park-like setting carpeted with pine-needle duff, gray moss, and grass already August yellow in spite of the recent rain. Red, pink, and white wildflowers dotted the landscape.

Sue knelt beside the trail and fingered some bright petals. "What kind of flowers are these?"

"I don't know."

"Really?" she answered, standing up.

"Really," I replied.

"You know," she said as we resumed walking, "at the beginning of this trip, I knew nothing, and you were supposed to know everything. I think I've learned a few things, but that makes several times now you've answered one of my questions with 'I don't know.' Your ivory pedestal is turning into a slippery slope, my dear."

"I don't know anything about flowers," I said, shrugging. "I can identify two flowers, roses and dandelions. But don't ask me what kind the roses are. As for dandelions, I always felt secure about them until someone told me there are two kinds. Since then I haven't even been all that comfortable with them."

"Not a man thing, huh?" Sue smiled.

"Not a man thing," I replied.

*   *   *

Having climbed the final ridge, we walked along a short muddy path to a viewpoint overlooking the falls. As if we had stepped over a threshold into a rain forest, the pines were gone, replaced by cedars, dripping with the moisture of a rainbow-laced mist rolling up from the canyon below.

After several minutes of silence, Sue turned to me. "I need some help," she shouted over the roar of the falls.

"With what?"

"I've been trying to decide how I'll describe this when we get home. It's so beautiful that I can't find the right words. *Spectacular, magnificent, lovely*—nothing's good enough for this. You're the one good with words. Give me some help."

"I don't think I can," I shouted in return. "You and I view these falls differently. You look with an artist's eye and see beauty. I look at these falls with awe, not at their beauty but at their strength. The power, the overwhelming dominance of the river taking on this eighty-foot obstacle. Scenes like this remind us how puny we are in the scheme of things. Just when we think we have everything under control, along comes a volcanic eruption, a tornado, a hurricane to remind us of our frailty. It's nature's awesome power I see in these falls."

"No," Sue shook her head. "That's philosophical baloney. This isn't frightening. It's beautiful."

"I didn't say frightening. Power's not frightening. It simply demands respect."

I moved next to her so that I could speak without shouting. "Tell you what. Sometimes the simplest words are the best words. You think the falls are beautiful. I think they're powerful. Maybe we should leave it at that."

"Okay," Sue agreed. "In fact, I think we can compromise."

"What do you have in mind?"

"We can say they are powerfully beautiful."

After a moment's thought, I answered, "Or we can say they are beautifully powerful."

Laughing, we leaned into each other. Then we quieted as if we had transgressed in church. We stood, arms around each other, and for a time became one with the falls.

*   *   *

I don't know how long we had stood silently watching and listening before Sue asked, "What were you thinking just now? You had a faraway look in your eyes."

"I was imagining what it must have been like for the first non-Native Americans who came upon these falls. Probably would have been some fur trappers for the Hudson's Bay Company. Or they might have been gold miners when gold was discovered in the Cariboo Mountains. Just imagine coming down the river and hearing this roar ahead of you. The fear, the adrenalin rush. Putting in and walking along the bank. And coming on this. Thanking your lucky stars you hadn't been daydreaming or so tired you'd not recognized the danger before it was too late. And then, looking into this canyon, knowing you'd have to find a way to get your canoes and your gear down there.

"Probably, though," I continued, "the first explorers came *up* the river, not down. And that wouldn't have been any better. You'd be at the base of the cliff, all this water pounding down on that jumble of rocks in front of you. And you'd be faced with the realization that you had to get your gear and canoes up here where we're standing right now. Just imagine it . . . ," I trailed off.

"You wish you'd been here, don't you?" Sue smiled.

"Sometimes I think I was."

"Oh," Sue said, giving me a shove, "Don't go all Hindu/Buddhist on me."

"You're right. I'm embarrassed. That was exactly the kind of thing people say when they want to sound mysterious or deep."

"I'm not so sure," Sue replied. "I know you think you'd have been at home in an earlier time. So if you weren't thinking reincarnation, you were at least thinking there are times when you might have preferred that life to the present. And to tell the truth, there are moments I think you belong in another century, too. But remember if you had lived then instead of now, you'd have missed out on the two most important loves in your life."

"And those would be?"

Sue held up one finger. "Basketball." Then she held up a second. "And . . . me."

"You're right," I laughed. "And one out of two is good enough to stay in this century."

"Need I ask which one?" Sue grinned.

"Well, I wouldn't choose the one that exposes my lousy jump shot."

Laughing, we retraced our steps along the muddy path and back into the world of lodgepole pines and wildflowers.

GIVE AND TAKE ON RUM LAKE

Sue and I had the campground to ourselves that night. The Boy Scouts had awakened us in the morning with their noisy preparations for an early start, and by the time we had finished breakfast, they were gone. Gus and Marge, the couple from Florida, had not stirred from their tent before we left for Cariboo Falls, but they, too, were gone when we returned.

We sat at the water's edge, watching the sun drop in an orange-purple sky. I lifted my Scotch. "Cheers, Babes."

"Cheers," she smiled as I clinked my glass against her cup of Tang.

"It's colder tonight," Sue shivered, snuggling closer to tuck her cheek into my shoulder.

"Uh huh," I agreed. "Fall comes early up here. It's already in the air."

"I'll be a little sad to leave tomorrow," she sighed. "I love this lake."

"What do you love most about it?"

"It's such a cutie of a lake," she began, "and . . . I don't know. I just . . . I'm going to miss it, that's all."

"Maybe it's the Paris Hilton," I suggested.

"You're right," Sue smiled. "If I could, I'd take it with us."

"Well, that'd be a first. I've seen canoes with sails. I've seen canoes with motors. But I've never seen a canoe with an attached outhouse."

I expected a laugh. Instead, Sue asked in an indignant voice, "Canoes with motors?"

"I know," I replied, agreeing with her tone of disapproval. "Incongruous, isn't it? It's like a marathon runner carrying a pack of cigarettes with him."

"Is that going to last the rest of the trip?" Sue asked, pointing to my glass.

"My Scotch?"

"I've watched you sip your carefully measured drink every afternoon, looking at it like a gift from the gods. But it has to be running low by now."

"This is day nine," I answered. "I've rationed everything in our food supply to last us fourteen days. That's more time than we'd need under normal conditions, but I always pad the supplies in case of storms, accidents . . . you know, all the things that might mean being out here longer than planned."

"So you took your little plastic glass there—with its cute little screw-in stem—and carefully measured out fourteen servings of Scotch before we left home?"

"Thirteen," I corrected. "The fourteenth day would be the last day. No camp that night."

I leaned back, holding up my glass to catch the sun's rays through the amber Scotch. We fell quiet, watching the shadows lengthen toward us across the lake.

"Why the concern about my Scotch supply, anyway?" I asked, breaking the silence.

"Well, I noticed this morning how light the food pack has become. And I thought probably we were running out of luxury items. I knew you'd pack enough of the essentials to last us. But Scotch? I wouldn't have figured that to be included in the extra-days rations."

"Luxury item? You think my Scotch is a luxury item? That's outright heresy. We may be in the wilderness, but we need our reminders of civilization. This, my dear," I intoned, holding my glass high before tipping it to my mouth for the final drops, "this is civilization at its finest."

"If you say so," Sue smiled. "Anyway, I hadn't realized how light the food pack was becoming until this morning. So I guess you were right when you told me it should be the pack I carry because it would get lighter and lighter each day."

"Seems kinda obvious, doesn't it?"

"Well, yes, but I don't mind telling you, I was doubtful as I struggled with it that first day when we had to do two portages. I was thinking to myself, 'Oh sure. We're going to eat this much food? Must be enough for an army in here.'

"But you were right again, of course," she smiled, patting my shoulder. "I paid the price early, and now I'm going to reap the benefits. All the rest of the portages are going to be a piece of cake. You, on the other hand," she grinned, "have just as much weight in your pack now as the day we started."

"You know," I said, trying to change the subject, "We'd better get back into camp and start dinner, or we'll be cooking in the dark."

"Okay," Sue agreed, standing up and extending a hand. But if I thought I had successfully broken her train of thought, I was wrong. "How many do we have left, anyway?" she asked, pulling me to my feet.

"How many what?"

"How many portages?"

"You mean how many total for the rest of the trip?"

"Of course, I mean how many total for the rest of the trip. What else *could* I mean?"

"Well, we don't have that many," I answered, turning away and stepping toward the campground trail.

"Wait a minute," Sue said, grabbing my arm and pulling me to a stop. "What are you not telling me?"

"What makes you think I'm not telling you something?"

"Maybe because I asked a simple question and you ducked it."

"What question?"

"Look me in the eyes," she demanded, taking my shirtfront in her hands and pulling me into her. "How . . . many . . . portages . . . do . . . we . . . have . . . left . . . on . . . the . . . trip?"

"Two."

"Two? That's all? Well, okay. Was that so hard?"

"Nope," I answered taking her hands from my chest and turning toward the campground again.

"And we have one tomorrow?"

"One what?"

"One portage," she snapped. "Do we have a portage tomorrow?"

"Well, . . . yes. We portage tomorrow."

We had walked only a few steps when Sue suddenly grabbed the back of my shirt, pulling me to a stop once more. I turned around. "What aren't you telling me?" she asked.

"What do you mean?"

"It's something about those two portages, isn't it? I'll bet they're really hard or something. Right? So hard my having a light pack won't help? That's it, isn't it? Those last two portages are brutal, aren't they?"

"Quite the opposite," I answered. "They're not hard at all."

"What is it then?" she demanded.

"Babes, I don't know what you want from me. We have two portages left, and they're not hard at all. Especially," I added, "now that you have such a light pack."

"So they'd be really hard if I had a full pack, is that it?"

"Not really."

She stared at me, waiting for more. When it didn't come, she shook her head and stepped ahead of me on the trail. "Okay," she said, taking the lead into the campground. "You obviously aren't going to tell me anything now, but I want you to promise some straight answers at dinner."

"How about *after* dinner?" I countered.

"Why *after* dinner?"

"Because I like a nice relaxed dinner conversation and this topic obviously has you stirred up. So we wait until after dinner when our stomachs are full and we are a good frame of mind. Then we can have a calm discussion of these things that are bothering you. It is," I added, "the civilized thing to do."

"You know," Sue said, stepping into the campground clearing, "that's the second time in the last half hour you've shown an interest in being civilized. Here I thought I was coming on this trip with a modern-day mountain man and, instead, find myself in the woods with a Lord of the Manor."

I laughed and pulled her to me for a light peck on the cheek. "Let's get dinner started."

"Okay, but you promise that after dinner you'll tell me about tomorrow's portage, right?"

"Right," I agreed and started for the bear cache to bring down the packs. "Oh, by the way," I said over my shoulder as I walked away, "it's not *one* portage tomorrow. It's *two* portages tomorrow." I didn't look back. But the silence behind me was deafening.

*   *   *

Sue circled the fire, trying to avoid the smoke. She had been at my left shoulder. Now she settled at my right.

"Smoke follows beauty," I smiled, lifting my coffee cup to my lips.

"Is that why *you* never have to move?"

"No, with me, it's a spiritual thing. I become one with the smoke, and the smoke, in recognition of a brother, gives me my space."

"Is this the way our marriage is going to be?" Sue asked.

"Meaning?"

"Anytime I ask a question you either can't or don't want to answer, you're just going to make up stuff?"

"I'm a creative person, Babes," I laughed. "Making up stuff is one of my best talents."

"Well, I'm ready to hear about tomorrow, and I don't want you making up anything. It's going to be really hard, isn't it?"

"No," I shook my head. "It's going to be fun. Different from anything so far on the trip."

Picking up a beaver stick I had carried up from the lake, I leaned forward to poke at the fire. A whirlwind of sparks spiraled into the darkness overhead. Sue pulled away from the stirred-up smoke and slapped my arm. "Would you quit playing with your smoke brother and get on with it."

"Okay," I smiled, leaning forward again to scratch a crude map in the dirt at our feet. "The hardest part of tomorrow will come right off the bat when we backtrack up the Cariboo River." I traced a path from my Rum-Lake circle, through the inlet from Unna and into the river. "Coming downstream, you don't realize how strong the current is, but you will when you paddle against it."

"So we struggle up the river . . . here, right?" Sue smiled, dragging a toe along the line I had scratched past the entrance to Unna. "I mean, this *is* the river, isn't it?"

"Right," I answered, ignoring her sardonic jab at my crude little map.

"And when does all this fun begin?"

"Right here," I replied, poking at a bend in my now-smudged river line. "This is where we enter Babcock Creek. We have to be careful to watch for the entrance, or . . ."

"It's okay," Sue interrupted. "You can call it Three Mile Creek if you want to."

"Really? Why the change of heart?"

"Last night I was talking to Stan, and he said he could tell we hadn't been married very long because we never seemed to disagree on anything. I told him how wrong he was. To prove my point, I described our conversation about how silly I thought it was to call a creek Three Mile Creek when it wasn't even close to three miles long. I asked Stan what he and Larry called it, and he said Babcock Creek."

"So?"

"Well, I thought I had an 'I-told-you-so,' but Stan went on to say the name had changed before they made their first trip up here or they'd be calling it Three Mile Creek, too. He said people like you who were here before a neat name like Three Mile Creek was changed to something as dull as Babcock Creek deserved the right to stay with the original name. I guess in his mind it's like having some kind of grandfather clause. Or," she grinned, "an old-timer's clause, something like that."

"And *that* convinced you?"

"Not quite. Stan gave me some marital advice that convinced me."

"Oh, really? And that was?"

"He said if I was going to be like most wives and try to change you—which, of course, I am—I should learn to pick my battles and arguing about the name of a creek didn't quality. He said if I give in on the small stuff, the big victories will come easier."

"Well, good for Stan, I guess. But if you want the truth, I never planned to change. When my mouth was saying 'Babcock Creek,' my mind was saying 'Three Mile Creek.'"

"Yes, dear," Sue smiled. "And won't it feel good, for a change, to have your mouth saying what your mind is actually thinking?"

"Right now," I replied, "it's a good thing my mouth *isn't* saying what my mind is thinking."

"Okay, then," Sue laughed. "Tell me what's going to happen on Three Mile Creek."

"Well, as I told you before, we'll need to line portions of the creek, and that's some of the fun tomorrow. With all the rain we've had, the creek should be running high, so we'll be able to canoe quite a bit of it. But we'll still have long stretches too shallow to paddle. When we come to those, we'll step out and line the canoe upstream."

"And that's fun?" Sue asked.

"It is. I told you that before. The canoe just follows us along, sometimes through less than a foot of water. We may have to give it a little shove over a gravel bar now and then, but that's about the only work we really have to do except for the beaver dams."

"Beaver dams?"

"Uh huh. There are some beaver dams that we'll need to slide the canoe over. But that's pretty easy, too. We have to be careful not to damage the dams because not only do they hold back ponds that give us deep water to paddle again but also because . . . well, they belong to the beaver. But we can manage to get the canoe over the dams without much trouble."

"Okay," Sue replied, "the creek does sound kind of fun, but what about the two portages? I know they're hard because you didn't want to talk about them this afternoon."

"At the headwaters of Three Mile Creek, we enter Babcock Lake. It's a short, easy paddle. The lake's only a couple of miles long. The takeout point is the start of our first portage."

"And it's two miles straight up and two miles straight down, right?"

"You couldn't be more wrong," I smiled. "It's a quarter of a mile at the most and flat as a pancake."

"Seriously?"

"Uh huh. That portage leads us to Skoi Lake, which is more like a pond than a lake, probably a half mile across."

"And then the second portage?" Sue asked, suspiciously. "Brutal, right?"

"Are you ready for this?" I grinned. "It's so short and so flat you can actually stand at the takeout point and look through the trees to the next lake. In fact, it's so flat and easy there's a wheelbarrow there. We don't even have to shoulder our packs. We just throw them into the wheelbarrow and wheel them over."

"A wheelbarrow?"

"Yep. Unless something has happened to it. But it's been there on all my other trips around the circuit."

"A wheelbarrow."

"Right," I grinned. "A real honest-to-God wheelbarrow."

Sue stared at me, frowning. "I don't get it," she said. "Why did you lead me to believe the last two portages were so hard?"

"I didn't, Babes. I told you they were easy."

"Yes, but you said it in such a way that I didn't believe you. I was going on about how right you were at the beginning of the trip when you said I should carry the food pack because it would become lighter as we went along. And then I was rubbing it in because your pack weighs the same as when we started, and you said . . ." Suddenly her face darkened. "Wait a minute! Wait just a minute! You conned me!"

"What?" I asked, assuming my most innocent look.

"The food pack would be lighter the second half of the trip? Right. What you neglected to mention was that there *are* no portages the second half of the trip."

"Well," I said, shrugging. "There're two."

"Right," Sue sniffed. "There are two. Both little strolls through the trees. Oh," she added, "and don't forget the wheelbarrow."

"While we're not forgetting," I reminded her, "my pack does weigh the same as it did when we started."

"Uh huh, fine," she replied. "Think you can get it into the wheelbarrow all by yourself?"

To keep Sue from seeing my grin, I picked up my stick again and poked at the embers of our dying fire.

"I'm ready to turn in," she announced, rising from our log. "Are our toothbrushes in the day pack?"

"What? Yes, they're where they've been the entire trip. In the day pack."

"Well, you know what?" Sue replied, looking down at me. "Tomorrow morning after I brush, I'm going to put my toothbrush in your big pack. Then your pack won't be just as heavy as it was the first day. It'll weigh *more*."

"Okay," I smiled.

"And I might throw in some rocks as well."

"Okay," I agreed again.

"And maybe I'll fake an ankle injury and make you carry me over the two portages."

"Well, actually I'd carry you over only one of the portages. Don't forget the wheelbarrow."

"So if I had an ankle injury, you'd just toss me into a wheelbarrow and wheel me over to the next lake?"

"A *faked* injury," I smiled.

"How can you be so calm when I'm trying to get a rise out of you?"

"It's a spiritual thing. When I feel a cloud of tension around me, I become one with that cloud, and my tranquility becomes one with the tension, defusing it into serenity."

"Blowing smoke again?" Sue asked, extending a hand.

"I'm a creative person, Babes," I replied, allowing her to tug me to my feet. "Blowing smoke is one of my best talents."

"Yes, it is, my dear," Sue laughed. "Yes, it is."

DAY 10

OPENED-TOED SHOES

I carried the two packs from the bear cache and placed them outside the tent. Pulling back the tent flap, I looked in at Sue's curled form, buried deep in her sleeping bag. "Hey, sleepyhead. Get up. We want an early start this morning."

"It's not morning yet," she muttered. "It's still dark."

"It may be dark inside that sleeping bag, but out here we have a blue sky and a warm sun. It promises to be one of the best days we've had since Isaac Lake. Now get up."

"Okay. Quit nagging. I'm getting up."

I carried the day pack to the fire pit, where I set up the camp stove to heat a pan of water for our oatmeal and coffee. Sitting on a log, I leaned forward, my chin resting in both hands, and tested the proverb about a watched pot never boiling.

"Hey," Sue called, her head jutting from the tent front. "Should I wear shorts today?"

"Yes."

"Yes? We're going to be wading the creek through the woods, aren't we? What about the bugs? Won't they eat us alive?"

"They're not as bad on the west side of the circuit," I answered, "but just to be on the safe side, we'll leave our long pants out instead of packing them. Then we'll have them handy in case we have to make a quick change."

"Right. Good plan," Sue agreed as she ducked back into the tent.

A few moments later, her head popped out once more. "So, if the bugs swarm us, I'm to walk around with my pants legs all soaked?"

"Unless you can figure out how to wade up a creek and not get them wet, yes, if the bugs attack us, you're going to walk around with your pants legs all soaked."

"Okay." Once again she disappeared.

"Hey," I called. "Don't forget you're wearing your tennis shoes today."

"Got it," she answered from inside the tent. "I remembered."

Sue and I usually canoed barefoot, whatever footwear we needed dangling by shoestrings from the middle thwart of the canoe, our hiking boots on days of portaging or rain and our tennis shoes on other days. Being barefoot made stepping into and out of the canoe easier. Also, in the event we swamped, not having to swim in shoes was an additional safety factor. But because in lining the creek, we'd be walking through gravel, mud, rocks, sticks—all the debris found on the bottom of a creek bed—we needed to wear shoes. And since we'd be continually stepping into and out of the canoe, we couldn't take off and put on our shoes over and over again. We'd have to wear our tennis shoes while we paddled.

The water had begun to boil, and I checked my watch, timing the necessary wait before it was safe to use. Behind me, Sue announced, "Here I am, shorts and tennis shoes, just as instructed."

I turned to see her standing at attention, her hands out in a crucifixion pose. "Ready for inspection, sir."

"Looks good," I said, "but I need your shoes."

"What?" she asked, dropping her arms.

"Your tennis shoes. Take them off. I need them."

"Why?"

"Do you always have to know why? Just give me your shoes."

Shaking her head, she sat on the log and slipped her shoes from her feet. "Here," she said, handing them to me. "But I'm warning you right now. They aren't going to fit *your* feet."

I swung a leg over the log to straddle it and placed one of the shoes before me. Pulling my hunting knife from its sheath, I plunged it into the toe of the shoe.

"Hey! What are you doing?"

"I'm cutting a hole in your shoe," I answered as I sawed a triangular patch from the toe.

"I can see that. But why?"

It's an old canoeist trick," I explained, dropping the first shoe and replacing it with the second. I stabbed through its toe and began my sawing motion once more. "We're going to be wading in the creek and stepping in and out of the canoe over and over again. When we do, your shoes are going to fill with water. And then they'll get heavy, and you'll be stepping out of them. These holes are for drainage. Every time you kneel to paddle, the water will run out through the holes."

"But you're ruining my shoes," Sue complained.

I held up the second shoe, a scuffed, stained, frayed survivor of nine days on the circuit. "Were you really planning to wear this once we return home?"

"Probably not," Sue grinned, sheepishly. "But I *was* planning to wear it the rest of the trip."

"And you will," I agreed, beginning to saw at the shoe once more. "These shoes will be better than they were before—at least as far as canoeing is concerned."

"Well, I hope you're doing the same thing to yours," she sniffed. In answer, I held up a foot, wiggling my big toe through the newly sliced hole.

"Here," I said, holding out her shoes. "Believe me, these will be better."

"I suppose," Sue pouted, sliding a foot into one of the shoes. "What's for breakfast?

"Oatmeal."

"Oh," she sighed, slipping on the second shoe, "I'm really getting tired of oatmeal."

"Oatmeal's good for you," I answered, rising to remove the pan from the stove. "It'll grow hair on your chest."

"I don't want hair on my chest."

"In that case, it'll take hair off your chest."

"I don't have hair on my chest."

"Are you going to be argumentative all morning just because I cut holes in your shoes?"

"Are you going to be smug just because you did?"

"Tell you what," I replied, tearing the corner off one of the instant-oatmeal packets and pouring it into a bowl. "I'll let you in on something that'll make you feel good."

"Oh?" Sue asked. "What?"

"If all goes well, we'll camp tonight at Pat Point. It's a big, popular campground on Spectacle Lake. Probably some of the people who were on Unna yesterday will be there. It could be crowded, but because it's such a big campground, we should be able to find a space. And you, my dear, will have ample opportunity to mingle to your little heart's content."

"You promise?" Sue brightened.

"Well, I can't promise. But I've camped there every time I've been up here, and it's always been full of people. With the crowd we've been leapfrogging the last few days, I think the campground could have the most people we've camped with since Isaac Lake."

"And I'll have time to socialize?"

"We should be there by early afternoon at the latest. You'll have more time than even *you* need to become best friends with everyone in the campground."

"I don't know," she grinned. "They might not warm up to someone with holes in her shoes."

"Oh, I think they will, Babes. I think they will."

Lining Three Mile Creek

LUNCH BREAK ON SPECTACLE
LAKES WITH AN *S* . . . PLURAL

I stepped from the trees shading the trail from Skoi Lake and looked down the gentle slope to the sandy shore of Spectacle Lakes. Sue, her back to me, knelt by our camp stove pouring our last packet of Top Ramen into a pan of boiling water. I watched as she reached for her favorite stirring tool, a peeled beaver stick she had lovingly carried all the way from Isaac Lake. "It's the perfect shape and size," she had announced the first day she used it. *She's probably planning to take it home and use it in our kitchen*, I thought. *I can just imagine the looks on faces of dinner guests who wander into the kitchen and see Sue using a stick to prepare their meal.*

The promise of the morning sun had held. Sparkles of sunlight danced on the surface of the lake. Overhead, a hawk circled, pestered by a small dark bird dive-bombing the hawk over and over again, darting, changing direction at the last possible moment to avoid collision. The hawk, seemingly unimpressed, glided in ever-widening circles. I watched until the dive bomber broke off the attack and flew toward the trees on the western ridge.

I started down the slope toward Sue. Halfway there, I slipped, sending a scree of pebbles and dirt clods ahead of me down the trail. My feet shot forward, throwing me on my back. I slid several feet before coming to an ignominious stop. When I sat up, I fully expected to hear Sue laughing, but with back still turned, she calmly stirred the soup, seemingly unaware of my mishap.

Dusting myself off, I stepped from the trail onto the sandy beach. As I neared Sue, she said, without looking back, "I assume that's you trying to sneak up on me."

"I wasn't trying to sneak up on you," I replied, kneeling beside her. "And need I remind you the last time you made that assumption on a beach, you found yourself face to face with a hairy beast?"

Sue reached over and ran the back of her hand down the ten-day growth on my cheek. "Déjà vu all over again," she smiled.

"Yogi Berra," I replied.

"Yogi Bear?"

"No, Yogi *Berra.* 'Déjà vu all over again' is a Yogiism."

"Oh, right," Sue grinned. "I thought you were still talking about the bear."

She held out her stick, a couple of dripping noodles hanging from it. "Want to test these to see if they're done?"

I picked a noodle from the stick and sucked it into my mouth. "Perfect," I said, nodding.

A few minutes later we sat leaning against a lakeside log, dipping our camp spoons into cups of Top Ramen. "So this is Spectacle Lake," Sue said, looking over the water.

"Actually, if you believe the map, it's Spectacle *Lakes,* plural."

"There's more than one Spectacle Lake?"

"Not as far as *I* can tell," I answered. I pointed down the lake with my spoon. "From here to Bowron River, it's a straight shot for twelve and a half miles. But for some reason, the map divides this lake into sections with different names. The lower section is called Spectacle Lakes with an *s* . . . plural. The upper section is called Swan Lake without an *s* . . . singular."

"You have no idea why a lake has more than one name?"

"Not the foggiest."

"Come on. There has to be some separation into different parts somewhere."

"Well," I said, "Pat Point is about four or five miles from here. The Point is a promontory stretching from the west side of the lake. On the east side is a smaller promontory. So if we were going on instead of stopping at Pat Point, we'd jog a little to the right and then to the left, but as far as I'm concerned, this is all one lake."

"What about Swan Lake?"

"Haven't a clue. We'll be paddling along, and Spectacle Lake will simply become Swan Lake."

"Spectacle *Lakes* . . . with an *s* . . . plural," Sue corrected.

"Right. Spectacle Lakes . . . with an *s*," I repeated.

"*Plural*," Sue emphasized.

"Plural," I agreed.

"I love correcting an English teacher," Sue grinned.

"I'm sure you do."

"Anyway," she said, leaning over to take my cup and put it aside with hers, "you got the wheelbarrow back to Skoi Lake okay?"

"Sure. Tucked it under the big lodgepole pine, right where we found it."

"And you managed that with only one major tumble down a hill," Sue smiled.

"Oh, you saw that."

"Of course, I saw that," she laughed. "I'm alone in bear country, and I hear a large mammal rolling down a hill behind me. You think I'm not going to turn around to see what's going on?"

"I wasn't rolling. I was skidding."

"Okay. I hear a large mammal *skidding* down a hill behind me, and you think . . ."

"All right, already! How come you weren't laughing when I came to?"

"In the first place, you weren't knocked out, so don't try to get some sympathy from me that way. In the second place, I love you. Far be it for me to damage your macho image of yourself."

"Well," I smiled, "thank you for that."

"You're welcome," she replied, extending her hands above her head in a full upper-body stretch.

"You know," she continued, relaxing against the log once more, "this morning has really been fun. When you told me I'd have a good time pulling the canoe up a creek, pushing it over beaver dams, and crossing two lakes with portages in between, I thought you were sugarcoating things to make me feel good. But what made me think you *might* really be telling the truth was the wheelbarrow. Even you, with your crazy imagination, couldn't make up anything as goofy as a wheelbarrow up here in the middle of nowhere."

"Is that a compliment?"

"I'm not sure," she smiled. "Anyway, this morning was everything you said it would be. Lining the canoe up the creek was fun. I loved the way it just trailed along behind us. And those small lakes—especially cute little Skoi—the flat, easy portages . . . Everything was great.

"Getting the canoe over the beaver dams was a little hard," she continued, "but even that wasn't too bad. I wish we'd seen a beaver, though. But I don't think they live there anymore."

"Why not?"

"Because we didn't see any houses."

"Houses?"

"Yes, those piles of sticks and mud they live in."

"Oh, you mean lodges. They're called beaver lodges, not houses."

"Okay, lodges. Anyway, there weren't any in the pools."

"That doesn't mean there are no beavers there, Babes. Contrary to what many people believe, beavers don't always build lodges. When I was running my trap lines, I seldom came upon lodges. Usually, they build dens in the banks along rivers or streams. I think they actually prefer those to lodges. I found lodges only in places where sturdy banks weren't available—marshes, swamps, areas like that.

"But we'll probably see some lodges on Bowron River. The lower part of the river meanders through flooded lowlands, a slow-moving current through a swampy, marshy area. We might even see some beaver there. It's a great place to spot wildlife."

"I'm disappointed," Sue replied. "I had this idea of these smart animals building little castles of mud and sticks, and now you tell me they would rather live in a hole in a riverbank?"

"Don't ever think beavers aren't smart," I objected. "And the dens aren't just holes in a bank. They start a tunnel below the surface of the water and angle it upward until it clears the water level by a couple of feet or so. Those tunnels run as far as fifty feet inland sometimes. Then they build a chamber with at least one escape tunnel in addition to the main tunnel. They scatter wood chips to keep the floor of the chamber dry and poke air vents through the ground cover above.

"The beaver is amazing," I continued. "As far as I know, it's the only animal except man that alters its environment to fit its lifestyle. All other animals adapt their lifestyles to the environment. Beavers build dams. They build canals to move building material and food to the water. They build special rooms to store food for the winter. They build mud slides on the banks so that if they're threatened, they can shoot down the slides into the water. And the kits," I smiled, "the kits play on these slides just like human children in playgrounds."

"The kids?" Sue asked.

"No, the kits. That's what baby beavers are called.

"And don't even get me started on their physical makeup," I continued. "In addition to their normal eyelids, they have a third, an inner eyelid that's transparent. They can see through it when they swim under water, sort of like a pair of swimming goggles we might use. Their ears and nostrils completely close when they swim, and they have folds of skin behind their teeth that they can pull shut over their throat passages when they gnaw wood underwater and even on land. That way water or splinters don't go down their throats. And they waterproof their outer coats of fur by . . ." I stopped midsentence when I saw Sue's amused grin. "Sorry. Guess I got on a roll."

"No, I'm loving it. Why don't I put on some water for coffee? We can have a couple of fig bars for dessert, and you can tell me more. I mean, it's early, isn't it?" She reached over and turned my wrist to check my watch. "See. It's just past noon. We don't have to leave yet, do we?"

"We should," I answered. "Remember, I promised you an early arrival at Pat Point so you could socialize with the crowd that's usually there."

"I don't need that crowd. I'm enjoying the socializing I have going on right now."

"Huh? What . . . ? You mean me? Socializing with me?"

"I mean you. When you get excited about something like this, I really enjoy being around you."

"That's great, Babes, but I really think we should get going. It won't take us more than an hour or so to reach Pat Point, and getting there early will let us can grab a good campsite before others arrive."

"Well, okay, I guess, "Sue said. "But you have to promise you'll tell me more about beavers tonight."

"I promise," I answered, coming to my feet and extending a hand. She picked up our cups and allowed me to pull her up.

As we started toward the canoe, Sue took my arm. "Maybe you'd better hold on to me," she suggested.

"Why?"

"There's a slight incline here, and I wouldn't want you to go rolling—oh, sorry, I mean *skidding*—I wouldn't want you to go skidding into the lake."

"I see," I said, taking her wrist and pulling her into my side. "The be-nice-to-Bob time is over, is it?"

Grinning, she broke loose and moved ahead of me. "No," she said over her shoulder. "Never over. Just occasionally on hold." Giggling, she broke into a trot down the hill.

"'Never over. Just occasionally on hold,'" I repeated, smiling as I watched her near the canoe. "Now how cute is that?"

WEST-SIDERS

My prediction of a crowded Pat Point campground proved true. From a distance as we paddled up the lake, we could see a scattered collection of canoes along the bank above the takeout point. At the waterline stood a thin figure dressed in a light T-shirt and shorts. He studied us through a pair of binoculars. When he dropped his arms, Sue said, "I think that's Larry."

I leaned forward for a better look over Sue's shoulder. "I think you're right. Funny, I never realized how skinny he is. I guess I've never seen him in shorts."

"Well," Sue answered, "Since *we're* both wearing shorts, I'd not be critical of how others look in them if I were you."

"Just an observation," I muttered.

Larry lifted his binoculars once more and then abruptly turned and walked into the campground. "That's strange," Sue remarked. "He didn't wait for us. I wonder if something's wrong."

"Maybe he's embarrassed about his shorts."

"Right," Sue replied. "I know if *I* saw someone with your fine taste in clothing approaching me, I'd certainly scurry away to dress in something more stylish."

* * *

Five minutes later, we stepped from the canoe and pulled it onto the beach. Sitting in the sand, we tugged on our hiking boots. Our tennis shoes, soaked from lining Three Mile Creek, dangled by their shoestrings from the middle thwart. From behind us, someone asked, "Hey, you two, you staying here tonight?" We turned to see Larry and Stan, on the bank above us.

"Yeah, we are," I answered, coming to my feet. "How about you?"

"No," Stan replied. "We just stopped for lunch. We're moving on."

"Too crowded?" I motioned toward the canoes along the bank.

"It's crowded," Stan agreed. "But that's not really it. There's an old cabin on Bowron River where we like to stay for our last couple of days. Most people are in a hurry to get home by that point, so we usually have the place to ourselves. Gives us a chance to sort out our gear. And the river's good fly-fishing."

"When I saw you two coming up the lake, I kinda figured you planned to stay here," Larry added. "And since the campsite we used for lunch is one of the best ones left, I went in to tell Stan not to pack up our stuff until you got here. There's a group that came in after us who've been eyeing our spot."

"Yeah, it's been like a restaurant with a waiting line," Stan added. "You're sitting there, trying to enjoy your coffee after a high-priced meal, and the people in front of the line are staring at you, trying to make you feel guilty so you'll leave. It would've worked, too, if Larry hadn't come back and told me you were coming. We left our lunch stuff there to hold the place."

"But there *are* a couple of other campsites open," Larry offered. "So if you like them better, you don't have to stick with the one we saved."

"Tell you what," I replied, bending to the canoe to loosen the ties over our packs. "Why don't you two take Sue on a tour, let her make the decision. I'll stay here and unload our gear."

"Are you sure?" Sue asked.

"Positive. You go ahead. Pick us out a good spot."

"Larry can show Sue around the campground," Stan suggested. "I'll stay to help you with your packs."

"Come on, Larry," Sue smiled, taking him by the arm. "Give me the grand tour."

As they walked away, I said in a low voice to Stan, "She's anxious to start meeting people in the campground."

"I know," he said, nodding. "I've seen her work her magic. They'll be eating out of her hand in no time."

*　　*　　*

Thirty minutes passed before Sue and Larry returned. After stacking our packs and loose gear near the overturned canoe, Stan and I had stretched out on the sun-warmed bank, looking upward at a cloudless sky. Our conversation had drifted into silence, and I had started to nod off when Sue and Larry emerged from the trees. "We're back," she announced.

"Find a good place?" I asked, sitting up.

"Oh, the one Larry and Stan held for us is good enough," Sue replied. However, there was something in her voice—or rather something missing from her voice—that gave me concern. Her answer had been too flat, too matter-of-fact. I had expected her to return bubbling with excitement over the crowd in the campground. Instead, she was unusually quiet.

"What's wrong?" I asked.

"Nothing . . . Well, yes, something. I wasn't comfortable in there."

"Why not? I've always liked this campground. What's wrong with it?"

"There's nothing wrong with the campground itself. It's the people."

"The people? What kind of people would make *you* uncomfortable?"

"You'd have to see them to understand."

"Oh, really? Try me."

"Well," she began, "a couple of groups were okay. No one I recognized, but at least they looked like *us*."

"Looked like us? What did the others look like—Martians?"

"You'd have to see them to understand."

"You've said that. Now tell me what's wrong with them."

Blushing, Sue mumbled, "They're clean."

"What? They're clean?"

"Yes," she declared in a challenging voice. "They don't look like us. They're clean."

I glanced at Stan and Larry. They were grinning. They knew something I didn't know.

Turning back to Sue, I asked, "We aren't clean?"

"Well, we're not filthy or anything, but . . . look at us. We have grease and soot spots on our clothes. Our boots are scuffed and dirty. The people in there are wearing clean clothes. The men haven't shaved for a day or two, but they don't look like you three. Don't take this wrong, but you guys look like Ernest Hemingways gone bad."

"Now why would we take that wrong?" I muttered.

"There's a guy in there," she continued, "who's walking around in white tennis shorts. He has slicked-back hair, and he's smoking a pipe. A *pipe*, for crying in the beer! He looks like the leading man in an English comedy. And are you ready for this? I could swear I smelled barbecue. Hamburgers, if I'm not mistaken."

Throwing my hands up, I turned to Stan and Larry for an explanation.

"West-siders," Stan grinned.

"What?"

"I call them west-siders. Larry calls them short-timers. They're people who come in from the back side. They paddle the circuit backward from Bowron Lake to this point. Easy stuff. No portages. They can get here in a day. Then they camp for two or three days and paddle back to Bowron Lake again."

"Some of them make it all the way down to Unna," Larry added. "Remember those kids swimming when you two arrived at the lake? Those were short-timers."

"This is my sixth trip up here," I answered, "and this is the first time I've heard of west-siders or short-timers or whatever you call them."

"Well," Stan said, removing his hat to run a hand through his hair, "you told me you've spread your trips over fifteen years. Maybe west-siding has become more popular recently."

I shrugged and turned back to Sue. "You don't want to stay here? Is that what you're telling me? And that's because people have cleaner clothes, smoke pipes, and . . . what else? Oh, yeah, . . . barbecue."

"She's right, you know," Larry interrupted. "One bunch has a portable barbecue, briquettes and everything. They're cooking hamburgers for lunch. Drove Stan and me nuts."

"Probably a pretty good turn-on for any bears around here as well," I replied.

"To answer your question," Sue said, "I felt uneasy, kind of like an outsider or poor cousin. And that was embarrassing. But now that I know more about them, I *definitely* don't want to stay here."

"Why not?"

"When you and I came up here to do this trip," Sue began, "I'd have thought being what Stan calls a west-sider a big enough challenge. But not anymore. I've done the whole circuit. I've carried a fifty-pound pack over one portage after another. I've been bashed in the head. I've faced down a bear. I've been pushed down a lake by a wind that turned the canoe into a surfboard. I've run wild rivers and been kept up all night by an insomniac porcupine. *I've paid the price*," she declared in a raised voice.

"These people come in here and basically *drift* down to this place, where they hang out for a couple of days. I'm sure they'll go home and tell people they canoed in the Bowron Lake circuit, and everyone will assume they've done the whole thing. Well, they haven't. *They* don't have patched-up heads and tennis shoes with the toes cut out of them. "No," she concluded, shaking her head, "I don't want to stay here."

Stepping to her, I put my arm around her shoulder. "You're right," I smiled. "There probably isn't a single person in there with a patched-up head or tennis shoes with the toes cut out. So what do you think? Shall we go on up the lake?"

When Sue nodded a silent yes, I said, "Okay, then. That's what we'll do."

"You know that cabin on the Bowron River I told you about?" Stan asked. "There are a couple of decent campsites near it. Why don't you shoot for that? We'd enjoy your company, wouldn't we Larry?"

"What do you say, Babes?" I asked. "These two dirty enough to camp with?"

"Yes," she smiled. "They are."

"Well, guys," I grinned, "you pass the test. So I guess you'll have company tonight. Thanks for the offer. But go on ahead. Don't wait for us. We'll need to repack the canoe. We'll catch up with you later."

*   *   *

As we watched Stan and Larry paddle away, Sue leaned into me. "Thanks for understanding."

"Of course, I understand," I answered, pulling her close. "But tell me the truth. Do I really look like Ernest Hemingway gone bad?"

"No, you don't," she grinned. "In fact, sometimes you look exactly like . . . exactly like . . . Who's your favorite author?"

I could see where this was going. "Harper Lee," I replied.

"That's right," Sue said, snapping her fingers. "Sometimes when you're cleaned up and shaved, you look exactly like Harper Lee."

"Thanks," I grinned.

"You're welcome. Now come on. Let's get away from this place."

*   *   *

After ten minutes of paddling, I couldn't hold back my punch line any longer. "By the way," I said to Sue's back, "Harper Lee, that author I look exactly like . . . Well . . . Harper Lee is a woman."

"Why would you want to look like a woman?" Sue asked without looking back.

"I don't want to look like a woman. I just knew what you were going to say, and I was playing with your head. I like to stay a step or two ahead of you when you're being clever, you know."

"Oh, okay. But it's a shame, isn't it?"

"What's a shame?"

"It's a shame Harper Lee didn't write anything else after she published *To Kill a Mockingbird*." She gave me a moment to let what she had just said sink in before twisting around to smile at me. "So how's staying a step or two ahead of me working out for you anyway?"

I tried to maintain a straight face as she waited for my reaction. But I couldn't contain myself. I burst out laughing, setting Sue off as well. The sound of our laughter reverberated across the water, spooking a flock of swallows along the marshy shore. They exploded from the foliage and spiraled into the sky, where they circled as the flock gathered itself and then flew off up the lake.

And below, Sue and I righted our drifting canoe and followed.

A HUMPHREY BOGART MOMENT

Spectacle and Swan Lakes invite relaxed canoeing. Small islands and sandbars dot the shallow, warm waters. Along the shoreline, sandy beaches tempt canoeists to take frequent breaks. Nevertheless, Sue and I were surprised to see Stan and Larry standing by their canoe on a stretch of sand less than a mile above Pat Point.

"Wow, they didn't get very far," Sue commented. "Think something's wrong?"

"I don't know. There's a campground at the upper end of that beach. Maybe they've changed their minds about staying in the cabin on Bowron River. Anyway, Stan's motioning for us to come in, so I guess we'd better see what's up."

As we neared the beach, Larry lifted his binoculars to study an island across the lake. Stan moved to us and, straddling the bow, steadied the canoe while Sue and I stepped out.

In the meantime, Larry had wandered up the beach and, shading his eyes, stared at the island. Again he lifted his binoculars, leaning forward as if the additional six inches would bring the island even closer.

"Larry sure has a love affair going with those binoculars," Sue smiled. "What's he looking for, anyway?"

"He spotted what he thinks might be an eagle's nest with some little ones," Stan answered. "A bird that could have been an eagle flew off a snag as we were paddling up the lake. But we weren't close enough to be sure what it was. Then we spotted the nest, and Larry swears he saw little heads in it. I couldn't see anything from the stern. And we haven't seen any movement since then. But once Larry gets his mind on something, he doesn't give up easily. He'll probably be wading into the water for a closer look any minute now."

I assumed Stan was joking, but as if to confirm how much those two thought alike, Larry walked a few steps toward us and then turned and waded into the lake. "How'd you know he'd do that!" Sue exclaimed.

"Oh, I know Larry," Stan laughed. "The funny thing is he's afraid of the water. He'd never admit to that, and don't tell him I told you, but he is. He's stubborn, though. If he has to go into the lake to prove a point, he'll go into the lake."

"What point's he proving?" I asked.

"I made the mistake of saying I didn't think there was anything in the nest. So . . . well, you can see for yourself," he laughed, pointing at Larry, who stood mid-thigh in the water, studying the island.

"Where's the nest exactly?" Sue asked, shading her eyes as she looked across the lake.

Stan moved behind her and laying his arm over her shoulder, pointed toward the island. "Sight along my arm," he said. "Count three snags over from the left. See that tall one with the chewed-up top, the one that looks kinda like it's wearing a crown?"

"Uh huh."

"The nest's on the biggest branch on the left side just below the crown. It's right next to the trunk. See it?"

"Got it," Sue smiled. "I don't see any baby birds, though."

"Well, I hope they're there for Larry's sake," Stan answered. "Otherwise, he's liable to stand in that water till he's a prune." As we watched, Larry took two more steps into the lake, stood a moment and then ventured even farther, the water now almost to his waist.

Suddenly, he turned, grinning, and gave us a thumbs up. He began motioning for us to come to him, jerking his head toward the island. "He's definitely seen something," Stan grinned. "But I'm not going out there just to stand in that lake while he gloats. You two go ahead."

"What do you say, Babes?" I asked. "Want to do a little wading?"

"You know I would," Sue began, "but we'd have to put on our tennis shoes, and they're still soaked after Three Mile Creek. They'd be too clammy for me."

"Well, someone has to go," I answered, "so I guess it's up to me."

*   *   *

"What's wrong with *them*?" Larry asked as I waded toward him. "I can guess why Stan didn't come out. Didn't want me to be right. You know," he said, leaning forward and lowering his voice, "Stan's my best friend, but he doesn't like to be wrong—especially when *I'm* right. But what about Sue? I'd have thought she'd be excited to see some baby eagles."

"She wanted to—she really did. But she didn't want to put on wet tennis shoes."

"She didn't want to put on wet tennis shoes to wade in a lake?" Larry asked.

"I know," I answered. "Anyway, what do you have to show me."

"Oh, yeah," he brightened. Handing me his binoculars, he pointed to the nest. "Look at that."

I raised the glasses and, adjusting the focus, trained them on the nest. Balanced on the edge of the interwoven sticks, a fluffy bundle tested little wings. Behind it, two tiny heads appeared and disappeared, appeared and disappeared, almost in time to the cadence of their chirping drifting to us over the water.

"Whoa, that's cool, Larry. But what's stirring them up so much?"

He grabbed my shoulder. "Shh," he whispered. "Mom's coming." A large white-headed bird circled the nest, increasing the volume from the open mouths below. She landed lightly and, leaning forward, dropped something to the frenzied trio.

I handed the binoculars to Larry. After watching for a few moments, he lowered them, disappointed. "I know," I said. "It's not an eagle. It's an osprey."

"But," Larry brightened, "it's a really big osprey, isn't it?"

"Yes, it is," I agreed.

We turned and began wading back to the beach.

*   *   *

"It's not an eagle," Larry announced as we stepped out of the water. "It's an osprey."

"A really big one, though," I added in his defense.

"We could see the babies from here when she was feeding them," Sue replied. "Noisy little guys, aren't . . . What's that on your legs?" she interrupted herself.

I looked down. Both legs were spotted with slimy, black blobs. I turned to Larry, who was staring in disbelief at his own blotched legs. "Leeches!" I cringed, brushing at my thighs. "Get them off me! Get them off!"

"Wait," Stan commanded, stepping forward. "Don't pull them off."

"Oh, yeah," I shuddered, calming down. "You have to burn them, don't you?"

"No," Stan answered. "Just calm down. Their look is a lot worse than their bite."

"Is that supposed to be funny?"

"I grew up near a lake full of these little suckers," he answered. "My brothers and I got them on us all the time. I know how to get them off."

"Little suckers? Another joke? Come on. Quit fooling around. I want these things off me."

"Pulling them off can leave part of their jaws in you," he continued. "And because you squeeze them when you do that, they vomit into the wound. They do the same thing if you burn them. They'll come off, but their vomit puts all kinds of bad stuff into your system."

"Stan, I appreciate the lecture, but while you're dilly-dallying around, these things are sucking my blood. Larry," I called, "help me out here, will you?"

Larry didn't answer. And he didn't look good. His arms were wrapped around his thin chest. He was shaking as if extremely cold. Stan's demeanor changed when he saw his friend's condition. "Come here," he said. "I'm going to start taking them off Larry. You watch and then you can get them off by yourself."

"It's okay, Larry," Stan soothed, kneeling in front of him. Sue watched over my shoulder as Stan pointed to an especially plump leech on Larry's upper thigh. "They attached themselves at both ends," he began. "What you do is slide your thumbnail under one end like this," he demonstrated. "You can feel a kind of gristly circle. That's the suction cup. Get your thumbnail under it and just *pop* it up." The leech curled over, its lower end still sticking to Larry's leg. "Now do the same thing at the other end. Only this time, *pop* and *flick*. He jerked his hand upward, and the leech flew through the air, landing with a sickening, swishy sound on some pebbles in the sand. "Got it?"

I nodded and reached a shaky hand toward one of the leeches on my upper leg. I tried to work my thumbnail under the slick body, but I couldn't manage it. My entire life I had chewed my nails down to the quick. This was the first time I envied people who actually used fingernail clippers. "I can't do it," I said. "I don't have enough thumbnail."

"Well, *I* do," Sue answered, and without hesitation, she knelt and began removing the leeches, employing a kind of chant as she went along: "*Pop . . . Pop and flick . . . Pop . . . Pop and flick.*" In a few minutes, leeches lay scattered around my feet. I shuddered, watching them twist and squirm, coating themselves in sand as they searched for water.

"How you two doing?" Stan asked, kneeling by Larry, the two of them surrounded by their own collection of struggling leeches.

"I think we got them all," Sue replied.

"Take off the shoes," Stan instructed. "You need to check the feet."

I slipped off my tennis shoes and, leaning on Sue, balanced on each leg as she ran her hands around my feet and between the toes. "Can't find anything," she said, looking up.

"Okay," Stan said, walking toward us. "Now we have one more area to check." He pointed to my wet shorts.

"What? You don't mean . . ."

"You gotta check," Stan replied, "and you can't do it alone. At least," he grinned, "not unless you have a really big mirror. Tell you what. Larry and I are going up into the brush. We'll leave you two here on the beach."

I watched the two of them disappear over the bank and then turned to Sue. "All right, big boy," she grinned, "drop 'em."

*   *   *

Twenty minutes later, Larry and I sat on the beach, dabbing our wounds with hot towels, soaked in water from a kettle on our camp stove. I lifted my towel, checking a small trickle of blood from one of the bites.

"The bleeding will go on for a while," Stan commented. "Leeches secrete an anticlotting enzyme into the bloodstream. That's why they're sometimes used in medical procedures even today.

"Oh, and this is interesting," he continued. "The reason you couldn't feel them when they attached themselves? They spray a numbing anesthetic before they probe. They're actually pretty unique creatures, aren't they?"

"Unique?" I asked. "What do you think, Larry? You find those slimy little bloodsuckers unique?"

For the first time since we had stepped from the lake, Larry smiled. "Unique? No, myself, I wouldn't say unique. But my buddy here," he said, pointing to Stan, "picked those creepy things off me without even flinching. So if he wants to call them unique, well, I'm not gonna argue with him. And, by the way," he added, "your bride there did the same thing. So you and I can thank our lucky stars these were the two people who were with us when we needed them. Oh, and one more thing," he added. "I want to get off this bloody beach right now."

*　　*　　*

Once again, Sue and I watched Stan and Larry paddle away from us. "How's the bleeding coming?" she asked as we relaxed on the sand once more.

"I think it's finally stopping," I answered, dabbing at the wound again.

Suddenly, Sue, covering her mouth, began to giggle.

"What's so funny?"

"There's a movie with Humphrey Bogart and Katharine Hepburn where they're taking a boat down a river in Africa."

"*The African Queen*," I said, nodding.

"Right. *The African Queen*. Anyway, there's that scene where Humphrey is pulling the boat through a swamp, up to his neck in cruddy water. And when he climbs back into the boat, he's covered with leeches. Well," She smiled, "your face when you first saw those leeches on you was exactly like Humphrey Bogart's at that moment."

"I think he won an Oscar for that movie," I commented.

"If you're expecting acclaim for the way *you* handled the situation," Sue laughed, "don't hold your breath. Now come on. Let's catch up with Stan and Larry before they find another reason to stop. I don't know about you, but I've had enough excitement for one day." She stood up and reached down to pull me to my feet.

"By the way," I said, putting my arms around her, "Larry was right. Thanks for pulling those things off me. That went way beyond the call of duty."

"For better or worse," Sue smiled, kissing me lightly. "For better or worse."

GETTING IN TOUCH WITH MY FEMININE SIDE

Shadows from the west bank of Swan Lake had begun to lengthen across the water. "We need to pick up the pace, Babes," I called to her. "The entrance to Bowron River is sometimes a little tricky to spot, and I want to have plenty of sunlight when we get there."

"Why would the mouth of a river be hard to find?" she asked.

"It's not the mouth of the river," I replied. "The river runs west out of those mountains to our right and then turns north and heads for Bowron Lake. We'll be hitting the river about two and a half miles above the place where it enters the lake. *That's* the mouth of the river. What we have to look for is a channel connecting Swan Lake to the river. Remember I told you Bowron River is little more than a slow-flowing channel through a large marshy area? Well, there are all kinds of openings along that marsh, and when the water is high, they look pretty much the same."

"But it'll be marked with orange paint, won't it?"

"Yeah, but if we lose good light, we might have trouble seeing the post."

"Got it. How's this?" she asked, increasing the pace.

"Works for me," I replied, sliding into the new rhythm.

A few minutes later, Sue called back, "Did you ever have trouble finding it?"

"Finding what?"

"The entrance to the river. When you were talking about how easy it was to miss, I figured you were speaking from past experience."

I smiled at how easily she was beginning to read me, even with her back turned. "Yes, I did. The third or fourth trip up here, I paddled up the wrong channel. It got narrower and narrower until it finally just petered out. When the canoe hung up on a mud bar, I had to get out and push it.

But when I stepped down, I sank to my knees in slimy, smelly muck. No, let me qualify that. My *right* leg sank into the mud. My *left* leg hung up on the canoe. I finally worked it loose, and then I was buried to both knees. I had a devil of a time getting out of the mud and backing the canoe out of the channel."

Laughing, Sue looked over her shoulder at me. "I don't know why you keep coming up here. Leeches latch onto you, mud tries to suck you under—You're simply a catastrophe waiting to happen."

"Remember, it's the unexpected that makes the trip fun, Babes. Of course, things like blood-sucking leeches and leg-sucking mud are more fun in the later telling than they are in the immediate experience."

"I suppose," she answered. "But let me warn you, if we miss that river and end up in a swamp, I'm not leaving the canoe. Anyone steps out into the muck, it's going to be you."

*   *   *

We had paddled in silence for another ten minutes before I announced, "That's Pavich Island ahead."

"That's an island?" Sue asked. "Must be a big one. All those trees. I would have thought it was a peninsula or something."

"It is big," I answered. "About a mile long. Once we clear the island, we'll be near the upper end of the lake. And we're making good time, so I don't think we'll have any problems finding the river entrance."

*   *   *

We had reached the halfway point of the island when Sue, looking at the cut banks overhead, asked, "What did you say is the name of this place?"

"Pavich Island. Probably named after someone. So many places up here are. But it has a couple of interesting other names as well."

"Like what?" she replied, lifting her paddle and turning to face me.

"Oh, no," I said, shaking my head. "We have to keep moving. We don't have time for idle conversation."

"How long does it take to tell me two names? Probably five seconds, right? We could already have been underway if you'd just answered. Two names. How hard is that?"

"All right, I'll tell you. It's no big deal. I just want to get to the river before dark. You know? Before dark?"

"Before dark. I know. You could have told me *ten* names in the time you've been stewing about it."

"Okay," I replied, resting my paddle across my lap. "Of the two names I know about, I think you'll like this one best. The place is sometimes called Maternity Island."

"Really? Why?"

"Pregnant moose swim over here to have their young. Both the mothers and the calves are vulnerable to wolf attacks during the births, but the wolves won't follow the moose into the lake. So the mothers give birth and stay on the island until the calves are strong enough to leave."

"Oh," Sue smiled, "I *do* like that story. Now tell me the other one."

"Well, you probably won't like this one as much. A long time ago this place was called Deadman's Island."

"Is this going to be a pirate story?"

"No. It was called Deadman's Island because at one time it was inhabited by a tribe of Native Americans and they all died in a single year."

"How?"

"An epidemic. What some Native American historians call the white man's gift."

"The white man's gift?"

"Smallpox," I answered.

She was silent for a few moments before saying, "I don't like that story. A few minutes ago, you were telling me the island was a place of new life, and now you're telling me it was a place of death."

"I don't especially like the story either," I replied.

"Let's hurry up," Sue said, lifting her paddle and turning to face the bow. "I want to get away from this place."

*   *   *

By the time we had passed the northern tip of the island, pulling into the upper waters of Swan Lake, we were both wet with sweat. Sue had set a blistering pace in her hurry to leave the island behind.

"Hey," I called, "can we take a break?" She lifted her paddle, and we glided to a floating stop.

Twisting around to face me, she said, "Sorry I reacted that way. The island spooked me after you told that story."

"Well, don't think about the Deadman story. You liked the name Maternity Island, so call it that. Let your feelings center on the first story."

"I hate to tell you this," Sue smiled, "but *sometimes* you get things right."

"Thanks."

"You're welcome. But you know what? I like the story about the mother moose swimming to the island to have their babies, but I'm not really so big on the name Maternity Island. It sounds like a hospital ward."

"Well, duh. A place to have babies? Hospital ward? What's the problem?"

"It's just too clinical. If I'm going to erase the Dead . . . that other story from my mind, I need something more fun, more bubbly."

"More bubbly?"

"Yes," she laughed. "More bubbly. I'll work on it."

"Okay, you do that. In the meantime, turn around and look up the lake. You see that long ridge of land jutting into the water ahead. There's a campground right on the point. We need to head left of the campground to hit the entrance to the river."

We hadn't gone more than fifty yards when Sue suddenly quit paddling and exclaimed, "I've got it!"

"Got what?"

"The name. I've got the perfect name to make me feel good about the island. You ready for this? *Baby Moose Island.* Now how perfect is that?

"Baby Moose Island? That's the corniest thing I've ever heard."

"It's not. It's perfect for the story of mother moose saving their unborn babies by swimming to an island to escape wolves. You'd understand that if you were a mother. You know, you really need to get in touch with your feminine side."

"It has nothing to do with my feminine side, whatever that is. Baby Moose Island sounds like a Saturday morning cartoon."

Abruptly, Sue turned and, without answering, began paddling once more. I fell into her rhythm, but when she remained silence for several minutes, I began to feel guilty. *I've hurt her feelings*, I thought. *And over a dumb thing like the name of an island.*

But then her giggles began to drift to me. "What's so funny?" I asked.

Sue raised her paddle, and once more we drifted to a stop. "You were right," she laughed, turning to face me again. "Baby Moose Island *does* sound like a Saturday morning cartoon. But that's not why I'm laughing."

"Then why are you?"

"I'm laughing because I keep seeing the look on your face when I said you needed to get in touch with your feminine side."

"I don't even know what that means," I replied.

"I know, my dear," Sue smiled. "And that just proves my point, doesn't it? Now," she continued as she turned forward once more, "let's go find that river you're so worried about."

As we paddled toward the head of the lake, I glanced back at the island. Shadows from the western shore of the lake had almost reached but not overtaken the island's banks. A lowering sun highlighted the deep firs. In the thickets along the shore, leaves showed early color on this mid-August afternoon. *September must be magnificent up here,* I thought. And then I realized how I was viewing the island. Its beauty had overshadowed its history.

It takes someone like Sue, I reflected, *to salvage an island like this, to save it from a moment of tragedy and lift it into a celebration of life. Deadman's Island becomes Baby Moose Island. The dead go away, and the babies arrive. Good job, Babes,* I silently said to her. *Good job.*

But I do *have one question. What in blue blazes is* a feminine side *anyway?*

BEAR TALK OVER SCOTCH

"You think it's grizzly?" I asked Stan as I knelt, studying the footprints in the muddy flat by the river.

"I'm sure of it. Look at the size. The length of the claws. No question. That's grizzly."

"I know they're up here," I answered, "but I've never seen one. I remember Larry saying the two of you have seen grizzlies on this river."

"Yes, a couple of trips ago, we saw two of them going after sockeyes."

"Are the sockeyes running now?"

"Mid-August? It's the end of the run, but, yes, there should still be some in the river."

"Well," I replied, returning to my feet, "maybe we better not say anything about this to Sue."

"Say anything to me about what?"

I turned to see Sue standing on the bank above us. "Oh, hi," I managed. "I thought you were at the campsite."

"I was. I came down here to help you with the rest of the gear. Just exactly what is it you don't want me to hear?"

"Nothing. Stan and I were just talking."

"About what?"

"Nothing."

"What were you looking at in the mud down there?"

"Nothing."

"Nothing? Just a couple of grown men fascinated by a stretch of mud on the banks of the Bowron River, is that it?"

"Yeah, that's it."

"Let me see," she answered, stepping off the bank and walking toward us.

"Okay," I said, giving in as she approached. "We were looking at some bear tracks."

"Wow! Those are big!" she exclaimed, kneeling and tracing her hand over one of the footprints.

"It's a grizzly," Stan replied and then ducked from the glare I threw at him.

"How do you know?" Sue asked, not looking up from her study of the tracks.

"The size," Stan answered. "Especially the length of the claws. Black bears have shorter, sharper claws. Grizzlies have major claws."

Sue placed her hand inside one of the footprints. "Look at this. The claws are as long as my fingers. So why didn't you want me to see this?" she asked, turning to face me.

"I didn't want to scare you."

"Why would I be scared? It's just another bear."

Just another bear? I thought to myself. *How far has Sue come in ten days?*

"Oh, no," Stan objected. "It's not just another bear. It's a *grizzly* bear."

"They're bad, huh?"

"Yes, they're bad. Fortunately these tracks are at least a couple of days old. This guy was here before the last rain. So I don't think we have anything to worry about. But if you're concerned, you're welcome to stay the night in the cabin with Larry and me."

"What do you think, Babes?" I asked. "Want to move into the cabin tonight?"

"Are you kidding? Mice? Packrats? No thanks I'll take grizzlies any day."

"Don't forget the bats," Stan grinned.

"Bats?"

"Right. That shelter we stayed in on Lanezi? When we went in there, we stirred up a really big bat. You should have seen Larry chasing that thing around with a broom until it finally flew out the open door."

"Well, that settles the question, doesn't it?" Sue replied. "Nope, I sleep in our cozy little tent tonight."

"Okay, then," Stan answered. "I'll leave you two alone to set up your camp."

"Just a minute," I stopped him. "You should know this is the best part of my day."

"Oh, really? How's that?"

"Because in the time between setting up camp and dinner, I have my Scotch."

"Scotch?" he looked at me. "You carry Scotch on this trip."

"Oh, yes, he does," Sue answered. "He has thirteen carefully measured drinks. Every afternoon at this time, he goes into some kind of trance, twirling his glass, sipping, sniffing, nursing that drink. It's almost obscene, if you ask me."

"Scotch?" Stan repeated as if he had not heard her interruption. "You carry Scotch on the circuit?"

"I do. And the magic number is *thirteen* drinks of Scotch. This is the tenth day and our last night on the circuit. That means after I have my afternoon Scotch, there'll be three drinks left. If you and Larry showed up after dinner, the three of us could share those."

"*I* like Scotch," Stan grinned, "but Larry—Larry thinks Scotch is God's gift to mankind."

"Of course, it is," I answered. "He is, after all, a munificent God."

*　　*　　*

As the campfire cast our shadows into the trees around us, Larry seemed mesmerized watching me carefully pour a glass of Scotch into his cup. Stan slowly swirled his own drink as he waited. Finally, I filled the glass for the third time. "Cheers," I intoned, lifting my drink.

"To friends," Stan answered.

"How's it going, guys?" Sue asked, standing up from the camp stove where she had knelt to put on a pot of water for coffee.

"How's it going?" Larry smiled. "Frankly, early in the trip, I wondered what Bob had done to deserve a lady like you." Raising his cup, he continued, "Now I know." He patted the log beside him, and Sue sat down, reaching over to squeeze his arm in answer to his compliment.

"I keep seeing those bear tracks," she began. "It would take a magnificent animal to make tracks like that. So, you guys, tell me about grizzlies."

"Oh, that's probably not a good idea," I objected.

"No, really. Tell me. How will I know I'm looking at a grizzly if I see one?"

"They're big," Stan began. "Much bigger than the black bears you've seen so far. And they're far more aggressive. When a grizzly wanders into a black bear's territory, the black bear changes residence.

"They have a big hump on their shoulders," he continued. "And, though, they can be different colors, they're usually some shade of brown. But the tips of their fur is often white and bristly."

"That's how they got their name," I interjected. "The mountain men said they were grizzled-looking. It was just a short step from there to calling them grizzlies."

Stan smiled and raised his cup, inviting me to take over. "Of all the terrors mountain men encountered as they came west—snakes, mountain lions—the grizzly was the most feared," I continued. "There are stories of mountain men not being able to stop a charging grizzly with direct hits from their rifles, rifles that could drop a buffalo from great distances. And grizzly attacks came so quickly and unexpectedly. A mountain man who had made the mistake of entering a grizzly's space without knowing it would suddenly see the brush erupt with a roaring grizzly in full charge. And then . . ." I stopped, realizing what I was saying to Sue, who just a short time earlier had studied a grizzly's tracks not fifty yards from where we were sitting.

"No, no," she smiled. "Tell me. This is even better than when you were telling me about beavers. I want to know . . . really."

"She wants to know," Larry added. "So tell her. The best mountain man-grizzly story is Hugh Glass. You seem to know a lot about mountain men. You know *that* story?"

"Yes. But that's not the story to tell now."

"It is *exactly* the story to tell now," Sue laughed. "I can tell from Larry's expression it's a great one. Come on, Bob. Quit babying me. Tell me about this Hugh Glass."

"All right," I answered. "But remember you insisted. Hugh Glass was a mountain man. He was in his forties, old by mountain-man years. On one of his trips west, he signed on with a large trapping company.

"On a scouting trip ahead of the main party, Glass surprised a grizzly sow with two cubs. She attacked, ripping and tearing at him while he fought back with a knife. His screams brought the two trappers who had been scouting with him. They fired shot after shot into the grizzly, managing to kill it. But Glass was mangled. The grizzly had ripped at his back until his ribs were showing. One leg was badly broken. Out there in the wilderness, no one could possibly expect him to live."

I looked at my audience, my storytelling side having kicked in. Stan and Larry seemed as entranced as Sue even though Larry, if not both of them, already knew the story.

"But he did, didn't he?" Sue asked, leaning forward. "He survived that attack."

"Yes, he did. But with no help from the others. They decided it was just a manner of time until he died and they didn't have that time. They had been relentlessly followed by a party of Rees, who had killed several of the trappers. So the leader of the company asked for two volunteers to stay with Glass until he died, bury him, and then catch up with the company.

"After the main party went on its way, the two volunteers dug a grave and waited for Hugh Glass to die. But as you said, Babes, he didn't die. He was on the point of death, but he didn't die.

"The two volunteers began to worry about Indian attacks," I continued. "He was bound to die, wasn't he? If they waited much longer, they'd all three be dead. So they took his rifle, his knife, his flint—anything of value—and left. When they caught up with the company, they told the leader Glass had died and they had buried him."

"That was a lie they'd live to regret," Larry interrupted.

"Yes, they would," I agreed. "He came to and eventually managed to drag himself to a stream of water. Later he saw a rattlesnake curled by the stream. He managed to kill it with a sharp rock. It was the food he needed to give him strength for what followed."

"He ate it raw, didn't he?" Sue shuddered.

"Uh huh. And after struggling to set his own leg, he began to crawl. He was over two hundred miles from the nearest fur company's post. He survived by eating bugs and roots. Finally he came upon a wolf pack that had killed a young buffalo. He waited until the wolves had eaten their fill and then crawled to the remains and ate what he could tear from it. That meat gave him the strength to stand. Using a forked stick as a crutch, he set out once more."

"But what about his back?" Sue asked. "You said the ribs were showing."

"Yes, he couldn't keep the flies from it, and eventually it was crawling with maggots. To prevent gangrene, He lay on his back over a log rotten log full of ants and let them eat the maggots from the wound."

"And then?" Sue asked.

"And then he lived. He was discovered by a Sioux hunting party, who treated his wounds and took him to the Missouri River, where he caught passage on a boat. It took him to one of the forts along the river."

"But what about the two who had left him to die?" Sue asked. "Larry said they'd live to regret leaving him like that."

"Yes, they did. They had committed several major transgressions in the eyes of mountain men, not the least of which was leaving a comrade without his weapons. When Glass recovered, he hunted them down. One of them was Jim Bridger, a man who would later become a legend himself. But at the time all this happened, Bridger was a mere teenager. The other guy was more experienced, and Bridger had given in to the older man's insistence that they leave Glass to die. Anyway, after Glass had confronted them in public, he was satisfied to leave them disgraced in the eyes of their friends."

"My offer's still open," Stan said to Sue. "You want to stay in the cabin, we have room."

"No," Sue smiled. "That isn't so much a story about the danger of grizzlies as it is about the courage of men. I think I'm finally beginning to understand Bob's fascination with the mountain man."

"Well," Stan replied, coming to his feet and stretching, "he does tell a good story. But it's time to call it a night. Thanks, you two, for a nice evening. We probably won't see you in the morning. We get up at daybreak here and paddle down to our favorite fly-fishing hole. But maybe next year? We're usually here about this time every August."

I looked at Sue, who showed no reaction. "I've never returned on a back-to-back trip," I answered, "but we'll think about it."

"You do that," Stan smiled. "You do that."

DAY 11

SILENCE IS GOLDEN

"**Ow!**"

"Shh."

"I stubbed my toe."

"Be quiet. You'll wake them."

Stan and Larry, true to their word, had arisen before daybreak and were making their way through the campground to go fishing. I looked over at Sue, who lay on her side, facing me, a hand over her mouth to stifle her giggles. As their footsteps faded, she whispered, "When I first heard them, I was worried about grizzlies, but grizzlies don't stub their toes, do they?"

"I doubt it. And if they do, they don't stand around talking about it."

"Well," she yawned, "now that the Laurel-and-Hardy show is over, I'm going back to sleep. Wake me when it's time for real people to get up."

"Real people?"

"Right. Real people, not weirdos who think fish don't sleep in."

"I'm not sure fish sleep at all," I began before realizing by her deep breathing that she had either already fallen asleep or was faking it in hopes I wouldn't start a conversation.

I gathered my clothing and scooted from the tent. The air was crisp under a gray sky. Heavy dew hung from the brush around our campsite. Shivering, I stepped into my pants, pulled my sweatshirt over my head, and crow-hopped into my boots.

While waiting for coffee water to boil, I wandered down to the river to check for any new grizzly tracks. There were none, but I did find a spot where a beaver had crossed a mud flat during the night. Farther on, I found tracks that confused me a little. They moved across the mud, entering a muskrat run through high weeds along the riverbank. At first, I thought it might be a small mink, but the tracks showed only four toes. Mink leave a five-toed track unless they're loping, and these tracks weren't far enough apart for that. Puzzled, I started back to camp.

The water was boiling by the time I returned. Carrying a cup of coffee, I strolled up the hill to the cabin for a better view of the river as it wound its way north toward Bowron Lake, the last lake we'd paddle on the circuit.

I sat on the porch and warmed my hands with the coffee cup. From behind the cabin, the sun peeked over a ridge, washing away the predawn gray with an orange-yellow sunrise. From somewhere in the marshes, a loon greeted the warming light. *The daytime animals are stirring,* I thought, *and the nighttime animals are finding a bed. Nature's version of space sharing.* I leaned back against a porch post and sipped my coffee. "Yes, I *do* love it up here," I said aloud. My voice startled a squirrel nearby into scolding me in his chirping, shrill voice.

"You're right, guy," I smiled, having spotted the squirrel on his branch, beady eyes boring into me, tail twitching. "This is *your* place, not mine. It's time I go home." Lifting my cup in salute to my noisy host, I rose and started down the hill to our campsite.

*   *   *

"I don't care how good oatmeal is for your cholesterol," Sue complained, looking into her bowl. "I'm going to need several months before I can eat another mouthful of this stuff."

"Tomorrow morning you can have an omelet, fresh fruit, yogurt—whatever you want."

"And tonight, I'm going to sleep in a real bed with clean sheets," she smiled.

When I didn't respond, Sue asked, "Are you sorry the trip is over?"

"Oh, I'm always a little sorry on the final day."

"I know," Sue agreed. "When I think back on the trip, everything seems so long ago. So much has happened, so much that no one in my family would ever imagine my having lived through.

"All the little things I used to worry about—grocery lists, rush-hour traffic, deadlines at work—all that kind of stuff seems so trivial now. Oh, I know these things will become important again and what I'm feeling right now will fade with time. But all I'll need to put things into perspective is to remember my experiences in these past ten days. Up here, life is pared to the bare essentials. And everything is lived in the moment. Yesterdays and tomorrows don't mean much. Everything is . . ." She stopped midsentence. "Wow, I'm really running off at the mouth, aren't I?"

I put my arm around her and pulled her close. "You know, Babes," I said softly, "you've fallen into the trap of wilderness experience. You've become a philosopher."

"Yes, well," she smiled, kissing me on the cheek and then rising from the log where we had been sitting, "this philosopher is anxious to find that soft bed with clean sheets, so what do you say we get this show on the road?"

*　　*　　*

As I tied the second of our packs into the canoe, Sue asked, "So, we'll see lots of wildlife on this river?"

"Good chance for some of the best on the whole trip. But, of course, like everything else on the circuit, it depends on circumstance."

"Circumstance?"

"We have to be quiet. Some of the animals up here aren't easily spooked, but the smaller ones, the ones we might not have seen so far . . . well, they spook easily."

"So we can figure on bears, moose—the big guys—but, if we're noisy, not the little cute guys. Is that what you're saying?"

"Right. Noise sets off most animals. The last time I was up here, I didn't see a single living thing the whole trip down the river."

"Why not?"

"Because a jerk in a canoe ahead of me sang at the top of his voice the whole way. I don't know if he was afraid of bears, if he thought he was the next Pavarotti, or he was just plain nuts, but if I'd caught up with him, I'd have whacked him alongside the head with a paddle."

"No, you wouldn't," Sue laughed.

"No, I wouldn't. But I had a good time thinking I might."

"Sounds as if I should be quiet," Sue smiled.

"That's what I'm saying," I answered.

*　　*　　*

I returned from a last check of the campsite to find Sue standing some distance from the canoe. As I approached, she held a finger to her lips.

"What's up?" I whispered as I neared her.

"We don't have to wait until we're on the river to see wildlife," she replied. "Something just jumped into the canoe."

"What jumped into the canoe?"

"I don't know. I caught it out of the corner of my eye. It was kind of a flash. And then I could hear it moving around the packs."

"A flash? That's all you have?"

"That's all I have. A flash."

I began a cautious approach toward the canoe. Suddenly a head popped up. Rounded ears. Beady eyes. Long, pointed face.

"Oh," Sue cooed, "It's a mink."

A slender, tubular body sprang onto the packs. The animal exposed its white belly as it rose from its haunches, studying us, whiskers twitching below a nose testing our scent.

"Not a mink," I whispered, "but you're close. It's a weasel."

"Really? How can you tell?"

"The coloring's different. And it's smaller. It's definitely a weasel. That makes me feel good," I added, "because I couldn't recognize its tracks this morning. They looked like mink, but they weren't quite right."

"I don't know," Sue objected. "It looks a lot like the mink on Isaac Lake."

"It's a weasel," I repeated, watching the animal lower itself to all fours again, its eyes glued on us.

Suddenly, it feigned to the left and darted to the right, jumping over the gunnel of the canoe and streaking into the weeds on the lower bank. Popping up, it turned to give us another look and then raced into the woods.

"Well, that's the end of his visit," Sue laughed. "How can you be so sure it was a weasel? I mean I trust you on stuff like this, but it looked like a mink to me."

"I've had personal experience with weasels. My grandfather had one for a pet."

"He had a weasel for a pet?"

"Right. Its name was Emily."

"This is the grandfather who taught you how to trap?"

"Right."

"The grandfather with the hook for a hand?"

"That's the one."

"Not those pinchers people have today? A real hook?"

"A real hook. An honest-to-God pirate's hook, just like Captain Hook in *Peter Pan*."

"He must have been quite a character," Sue mused.

"He was special," I agreed. "A bandit . . . but special."

"And the weasel?"

"He had all kinds of strange pets," I answered. "When he lived in Pendleton, he had a pet coyote, but the authorities made him get rid of it because it was killing the neighbors' chickens."

"Well, how about Emily?"

"Oh, I don't know if Emily killed the neighbors' chickens. I'm sure she would have, given half a chance. She just eventually disappeared. Everything in my grandfather's life eventually disappeared." Sue didn't respond. She understood I was speaking from the dark side of my memories.

"Anyway," I brightened, "when I think of Emily, I see her stretched across my grandfather's lap, belly up, while he runs his fingers over her, scratching, tickling, almost like playing a keyboard, both of them enjoying a moment not really meant to exist in nature's scheme of things."

"Okay, that's enough of this downer stuff," Sue demanded. "We have a beautiful morning, our canoe is packed, the river is calling, and you're becoming downright depressing. Come on," she laughed, slapping me on the shoulder. "Let's go."

*   *   *

"I'm feeling exceptionally good today," Sue announced from her place in the bow of the canoe after we had shoved off and were heading down the river. "Who knows? I may break out singing any moment." When I didn't answer, she continued, "Or, then again, maybe not."

Reacting to my laughter, she turned, eyes twinkling. "I knew I could cheer you up."

"How'd you like to see an otter," I asked, "or a bobcat, maybe a lynx—something like that—on our last day up here?"

"I'd love it. Are you promising me we'll see one of those?"

"No, but I'm promising you we absolutely *won't* see one if you don't stay quiet."

"Oh. Right . . . Mum's the word . . . My lips are zipped . . . Not a peep from me . . . Quiet as a mouse . . ."

"Will you *please* knock it off?"

"Of course, big guy. All you had to do was ask." Giggling, she turned back to the bow and began paddling once more. "All you had to do was ask."

BOWRON RIVER FUR AND FIN

The lower stretch of the Bowron River is narrow, winding between high banks with rocks and washed-out stumps scattered along muddy cave-ins. I had warned Sue that even though the current was slow in this meandering stream, we needed to be alert for sweepers and deadheads. So when she called, "There's something in the river right ahead of us," I told her to lift her paddle as I checked the canoe, bringing it to a stop. Gently backstroking, I stretched upward, trying to look past her.

"I can't see anything, Babes. What is it?"

"A pile of brush."

"A pile of brush? Is it on a stump or something?"

"No. It's moving."

"Moving? You mean floating down the river?"

"No. It's going *across* the river."

"What? Are you sure?"

"Of course, I'm sure. It's moving across the river right in front of the canoe. And it's picking up speed. Wait a minute. There's something behind it, something swimming . . . Oh, wow! You gotta see this!" she yelled.

At that moment, what Sue had called a pile of brush appeared on my side of the canoe, moving, as she had said, toward the far bank. But it wasn't what I had anticipated. I expected a haphazard tangle of limbs, vines, or uprooted debris. Instead, a well-organized bundle of willow branches passed by, held firmly in the mouth of a water-slicked, dark head. Behind the head, a brown back broke the surface. In the trailing wake, a paddle-shaped tail served as a rudder, keeping the animal on course as it raced to cross the river ahead of us.

"So you finally got to see a beaver, didn't you, Babes?"

"Yes," she laughed, "and so close I could almost touch him."

The canoe had begun to swing in the gentle current. I brought it around just as the beaver mimicked my maneuver, turning south and pushing its bundle of willows upriver.

"Where do you think he's going with those?" Sue asked, raising her paddle but hesitating with it held high as she watched the beaver over her shoulder.

"I suspect it's tonight's family dinner. They'll chew the branches into more manageable lengths and munch on the bark. Then they'll save the peeled sticks for building materials on their next project."

"You know," Sue smiled, "sometimes when you talk about beavers, it's only a short step to imagining them living next door, dropping in for visits, attending church, the whole ball of wax. Did you ever think about writing kids' stories?"

"Nope," I replied, beginning to paddle again. "Like most English teachers, I plan to write the great American novel someday."

"Oh," Sue laughed, turning back to the bow. "Well, hurry up and write it, will you? We could use the royalties."

We paddled in silence for a few minutes before she called back, "Do you think we'll see more beavers?"

"I can't say for sure, Babes. There's always the possibility, but they *are* nocturnal. We were lucky to see the one we did."

"Well, if I can't see another beaver, I at least want to see some of their houses."

"Lodges," I corrected.

"Right. Lodges. I want to see some lodges."

"There won't be any along here," I answered. "But farther on, the river widens with some channels running into little side ponds. If I remember correctly, there are some lodges along that stretch."

"Okay, then. Gives me something to look forward to."

"I'm not promising, you know."

"I know. But I'm lucky. I wanted to see a beaver, and I practically had one in the canoe with me. So if I want to see a beaver lodge, I'll see a beaver lodge. In fact, I'm so lucky we'll probably see a whole watery cul-de-sac of beaver homes before we're through."

Smiling, I shook my head. *She's such an optimist,* I thought to myself. *On the other hand, she* is *lucky. If she wants to see a cul-de-sac of beaver lodges, we probably will.*

* * *

"They look like giant goldfish," Sue observed, peering over the gunnel at the large torpedo-shaped bodies in the deep pool below. "Except they aren't gold or yellow. They're red."

We had glided into the pool a few minutes before, and Sue had immediately discovered the large fish milling below us. Some swam a circle or two and then continued upstream. Others nosed an underwater gravel bar, stirring up clouds of silt and sliding sideways across the bar as if scratching their sides.

"Okay. You going to tell me, or what?" Sue demanded.

"Tell you what?"

"What these are. What do you think *what?*"

"They're sockeye salmon."

"Really? I didn't know there were red salmon."

"They aren't always red. This happens during the last stages of their lives. Until that point they're colored pretty much the same as other salmon."

"Why do they turn red?"

"They hatch in the upper reaches of rivers like this—*especially* like this because they prefer spawning in streams with access to lakes. They stay in the spawning grounds anywhere from one to three years, and then they answer that strange call of Nature that sends them down the rivers to the ocean.

"There they spend up to four years before responding to a reverse call and battling their way upstream to the original spawning grounds. It's one of the most amazing things in nature to me," I smiled, shaking my head. "I have students who get lost when they venture into downtown Portland, yet these fish—with pea-sized brains, I might add—go up one river after another and arrive at the place where they were hatched up to four years before. It's truly amazing."

"But what about the red color?" Sue asked.

"That's a unique thing that happens only to sockeye salmon, as far as I know. As they make the return trip, they change into this red color when they leave saltwater for freshwater streams."

"Maybe it's Nature's way of giving them something back for the journey they're forced to make," Sue replied. "Because they're really *pretty* . . . in an ugly sort of way."

"Pretty in an ugly sort of way?" I grinned. "I think that qualifies as an oxymoron."

"Well, look at them. They look like something a committee put together. They have that beautiful red body and that ugly green-gray head.

Also, when some of them flip over sideways, you can see their faces with those hooked snouts. No," she continued, "The bodies are pretty. The heads are ugly. I think Nature plays games with these fish."

"The distorted jaws are part of the spawning process, too," I answered. "They don't look like that most of their lives. When they leave saltwater for fresh water, the males develop a humped back and their jaws and teeth take on that hooked appearance."

"Nature giveth, and Nature taketh away," Sue intoned.

"Oh, that's good, Babes. If I ever write a book about natural occurrences, I may have to steal that for a title."

"Let's see," Sue laughed. "So far this morning, we've determined you'll write three books." She raised a hand and ticked them off on her fingers. "A kids' story, the great American novel, and a book about the jokes Nature plays on us."

"No, no," I said, shaking my head. "I never agreed to a kids' book, and how did a book about natural occurrences turn into a book about jokes Nature plays on us?"

"Look below you," Sue answered. "Nature says to these fish, 'I'll give you a beautiful red body if you make a return trip to your spawning grounds, where you can lay and fertilize all the eggs you want.' But then she whispers under her breath, 'I'll also give you a humpback and an ugly crooked jaw, and I'll kill you shortly after all that spawning joy.' Don't you think that's one of Nature's cruel jokes?"

"You might be right, Babes," I chuckled. "But look at it this way. Their last acts are procreation, and they go out in a red blaze of glory."

Sue thought about that for a moment and then, smiling, answered, "And you accuse *me* of always seeing the bright side of things."

She looked into the deep waters once more. "Those ones who are stirring up the gravel—are they laying and fertilizing eggs?"

"Could well be," I answered.

"Well, that seems like a very private moment to me. I think we should leave them to their romantic endeavors."

"I couldn't agree more, Babes."

And reaching forward, we dipped our paddles into the river and pulled away toward the series of ripples that marked the lower reaches of the sockeye spawning pool.

SILENT GOOD-BYES AND BEAVER TOES

As the terrain leveled along the river, its banks disappeared in a marshy overflow of water. Following the orange-dotted signs marking the river's main course, we wound our way through a morass of soggy water plants, bramble-covered islands, and weather-beaten snags.

Side channels drained into ponds on both sides of the river. As we passed each pond, we studied it for beaver lodges, Sue because for some reason finding a lodge had become so important to her and I because—well, because finding a lodge had become so important to her.

But it was not a beaver lodge that caught our attention at the next large pond. "Look," Sue called, pointing across the water at Stan and Larry's canoe. Stan paddled from the stern, maneuvering the canoe along a weedy shoreline of broken snags and lily pads. In the bow, Larry worked his fly line overhead before gently laying the fly into sheltered shadows below the snags.

"Boy, he's good," I commented.

"Should we let them know we're here?" Sue asked. "Maybe say good-bye?"

"No, we said good-bye last night," I answered, not wanting to interrupt Larry's artistry with the fly rod.

But at that moment, Stan turned our way, probably having heard our voices carry across the water. He said something to Larry, who looked over his shoulder while he stripped line from his last cast. They smiled and waved at us. We waved back and then, returning our attention to the river, paddled around a sweeping curve and left the pond behind.

"They're nice guys," Sue commented.

"Yes, they are."

"Did we ever get their addresses?" she asked.

"No. I don't even know their last names."

"Is that the way it works up here?" she pouted. "Meet people today. Forget them tomorrow?"

"No," I shook my head. "Meet people today. Don't *bother* them tomorrow. Canoeists don't come up here looking for lasting relationships with other people."

"Then what *are* they looking for?"

"All kinds of things, I suppose. To test themselves in an environment like this. To live for a short time outside the eight-to-five box. I don't know. I'm no sociologist. Look, Babes. I understand how much you love meeting people, and I'm sure you've collected more temporary friends on this trip than anyone else in the history of the circuit. But the key word here is *temporary.*"

Sue was quiet for a long moment. Finally she offered, "I just wanted to send them Christmas cards. Would that be against your mountain-man rules?"

"Well," I laughed, "I'm pretty certain the mountain men weren't even sure when Christmas happened, let alone receive cards. They weren't big on calendars. But Larry and Stan, on the other hand, would probably be happy to get Christmas greetings from us."

"Well, it's too late now, isn't it," she said. "Come on. Let's get going."

*　　*　　*

Sue's sullen mood lasted for only a few minutes. "You should be on the lookout for those beaver lodges," I instructed, as the river continued to widen. "We're coming across more and more sign. From all this cutting, I suspect there's a good-sized colony nearby."

As we paddled by the next pond, she shouted, "There they are! Look! Across the water! Right over there! Two . . . no, three! See them?"

"I do," I grinned. "But you're missing one. Look left of those three. See all those smooth, slick trails coming off the bank. Those are beaver slides. There's another lodge just beyond them."

"Oh, right!" she laughed. "Four! I told you I'm lucky. I wanted a whole neighborhood of beaver homes, and I found one."

"Yes, you did, Babes," I smiled. "Yes, you did."

*　　*　　*

"So this is it?" Sue asked. "The final lake?"

"This is it," I replied. "Seven miles of paddling to the finish."

We were sitting on a gravel bar at the mouth of the river, looking down the length of Bowron Lake. I had insisted we take a break before the final stretch.

"We're so close," Sue sighed. "Why can't we just go on?"

"This is the third longest lake on the circuit, and there are no places to get off the water if we tire or run into trouble. It's better to take a little rest now."

"Okay," Sue answered. "I guess I'm just anxious to finish."

"I know. It's been a long trip."

"Yes, but I *did* see my beaver, and I *did* see some lodges. I don't know why that was so important to me. In the last eleven days, I've seen a mother moose with its baby, some mink, a weasel, a porcupine, two big bears and a baby bear, but somehow the beaver and the lodges were most important. I needed to see them."

"You're forgetting the leeches," I reminded her.

"Oh, right," she laughed.

We sat in silence for a few minutes. Small waves from the lake, driven by a northern breeze, washed up the gravel in front of us.

"So how many beaver families shared my pond?" Sue asked. "I figure at least four."

"No," I shook my head. "That pond had only one family."

"What do you mean? There were four lodges. We counted them."

"Lodges that close together belong to one colony, Babes, and a beaver colony is made up of a single family—father, mother, and two years of offspring.

"Beavers are extremely territorial," I continued. "Separate colonies don't share a small pond like that."

"But there were four lodges. Why would one family need four lodges?"

"A family can live in the same place for several years. Over time, they may build additional lodges. Sometimes a colony can have as many as twelve beavers. The female gives birth to a new litter each year, and the young live in the colony for two years, learning the life skills necessary for survival. After those two years, they leave to find mates and start their own colonies."

"What keeps other beavers from just moving into a pond and pushing out the rightful owners?"

"Beavers mark the outskirts of their territory, and most other beavers seem to respect these boundaries."

"How do they mark their territory? Do they chew little 'no-trespassing' signs on the trees?"

"Now who's writing kids' books?" I smiled. "No, beavers have scent glands. They mark their territory by secreting this scent on little piles of mud and twigs. And almost daily they go around their property and freshen up the mounds."

"It all seems too polite to be true," Sue argued. "I have to believe an occasional antisocial beaver travels into a marked territory just to test the system. How do the other beavers handle this claim jumper? Do they come to fight or what?"

"Well, they won't let this transgression go unanswered, that's for sure. In fact, that's how we used to catch them when I was trapping. We'd spread the scent of a strange beaver around our traps. When the resident beavers smelled it, they came to investigate."

"Where did you get the beaver scent?'

"What?"

"The scent you used to lure beavers. Where did you get it?"

"I don't think you want to know that."

"Yes, I do," Sue demanded. "Where did you get it?"

"Oh, you can buy it," I shrugged.

"Buy it?"

"Sure. It's in any store that carries men's fragrances. Right on the shelf beside Old Spice and English Leather."

"Come on," Sue laughed. "Where did you get it?"

"Well, Babes, where do you think we got it?"

"I don't know. That's why I'm asking."

"I doubt this is something you really *want* to know."

"Yes, I do. What's the big mystery, anyway?"

"Okay, then. When we skinned a beaver, we cut out its scent glands. After a few days of drying the glands, we cut them open and . . ."

"All right," Sue interrupted. "I don't want to know."

"I didn't think so," I agreed.

After a couple minutes, I asked, "Ready to go?"

"No. I don't want to end our discussion of beavers on such a dark note. Here's what I want you to do. Tell me a beaver fact I can bring up at my girlfriends' card games. We're passing around the carrot cake and the coffee, and I say, 'Ladies, did you know that beaver . . .'"

"What?" I asked. "A gossip fact for your ladies' night out?"

"No, not a gossip fact. A *phenomenal* fact. Something few people would know."

"I don't think I have such a fact at hand."

"Sure you do," Sue countered. "You're a walking encyclopedia of beaver facts. I want something so good that if I went on *Jeopardy* and there was a category on beavers, I'd win because I'd know this single fact."

"Okay. Let me think . . . All right. Did you know beavers mate for life?"

"Actually, I think I did know that. And if *I* did, every other contestant would know it, too."

"How about this, then? Beavers continue to grow all their lives. Most animals—including us—achieve a maximum size and quit growing. But not beavers. On the days they die, they're bigger than they've been their entire lives."

"Well, that's kind of neat," Sue agreed, "but it doesn't exactly knock my socks off. I want something that knocks my socks off."

"Try this," I offered. "Included in this lifelong growth is their teeth. That's why beavers have to gnaw so much. They need to wear down their teeth, or the teeth will grow so long and twisted the beavers will not be able to eat and will starve to death."

"Oh, that's just great," Sue answered. "Just what I need to impress the ladies at the card table—a picture of some kind of grotesque vampire beaver starving to death. Or maybe I can add a scene where my vampire beaver circles his territory, touching up his scent piles *while* he starves to death."

"Well, that *would* probably gross them out all right," I laughed.

"What I want is a fact I can share with my girlfriends. But not an ugly fact . . . What I want is a . . . a . . . ."

"Girly fact?" I offered.

"Right," she grinned. "A girly fact."

I looked over the lake, watching the high, streaky clouds move across the sky.

"Well?" Sue asked.

"All right, let's try this. Every beaver has a split toenail on the second toe of each hind foot."

"A split toenail? You mean like torn?"

"No, it grows out as one toenail and then splits into two—like a two-pronged fork."

"Okay, why would I want to share that with my girlfriends?"

"Because it seems like something the ladies would relate to. Beavers groom their coats with these toenails. Instead of two-pronged forks, I should have said they're like two-toothed combs. The beavers rake these toenails through their coats, taking out all the twigs, mud, and everything else they pick up mucking around in the stuff of their daily lives.

"Oh, and that scent I told you about? Well, they use these toenails to work the scent through their coats. Its oily substance helps waterproof them."

"Now *that*," Sue laughed, "is a beaver fact I can use at both the ladies' card table *and* in *Jeopardy*."

"Oh, good," I sighed. "Now are you ready to finish this trip?"

"Yes, I am," she smiled, standing up and extending a hand to me. "Come on. I hear that hot shower calling."

EXCHANGING CAMERAS ON BOWRON LAKE

"**Another portage!**" Sue exclaimed. "We have to do another portage! I thought we were all done with portages."

"It's not another portage. We just have to get everything up there," I answered, pointing to the top of the hill before us. We had just pulled our canoe onto the floating dock at the takeout point on Bowron Lake.

"Not another portage? Okay, then, how do we get our stuff up there?"

"You can see the trail winding up the hill. We'll make two trips. On the first one, I'll carry the canoe while you bring up some of the loose gear. Then we'll come back for the packs."

"And that differs from a portage, how?"

"Well," I offered, "technically a portage is defined as carrying boats and gear overland from one body of water to another. And since there's no body of water up there in the park campground, . . ." I let my voice trail off under the withering look from Sue.

Fortunately, at that moment she was distracted by something she saw on the lake behind me. "Look. A couple of canoes coming in."

I turned and, shading my eyes, watched the canoes approach us through the choppy water. "Anyone you recognize?"

"No, I don't think so," Sue answered. "Looks like two couples. But not anyone we've seen before. They've definitely done the entire circuit, though."

"Scrubby like us?"

"Right," Sue laughed.

"Come on," I said. "Let's move the canoe and our gear up the dock and give them some room."

"Wait," Sue replied. "I want to get some pictures before the dock gets overrun with people and all their stuff."

"More pictures? Babes, we need to give these people some room."

"It won't take a minute," she answered, rummaging through the day pack for the camera.

But, of course, it did, and before we could move the canoe, the couples had pulled alongside the dock.

"Hey, sorry," I apologized to the leading pair. "We'll get our gear out of your way."

"No problem," the man in the stern answered, steadying their canoe as the woman struggled to pull herself onto the dock.

"Here. Let me help you," I offered, reaching for her hand.

"Thanks," she said, as I pulled her up. She turned to Sue. "I want to ask you for a favor."

"Sure," Sue answered. "What?"

"Well, I saw you taking pictures, and I was wondering if you'd take one of us. We've been all the way around the circuit without a single group shot. It'd be a shame not to get one here at the end of trip."

"Okay, I guess," Sue answered, glancing at the camera in her hands.

"Oh, no . . . no. I didn't mean with *your* camera. With one of ours. Then if you want, we'll take one of you two . . . With your camera, of course."

"Oh." Sue smiled. "That would be nice."

BEAUTY AND THE BEAST

"**You okay here?**" I asked as I searched through my pack for the waterproof pouch containing my wallet and car keys.

"Sure," Sue said, leaning back against the overturned canoe by the shoulder of the campground road. "I'm fine. It's good to be guardian of the packs while you go on yet another hike."

"It's not much of a hike," I answered, straightening up, the pouch in my hand. "The parking lot's just up the hill at the top of the campground. I'll be back before you know it."

But as I walked up the gravel road, I worried about what I would find in the parking lot. On one of my trips, I had arrived at my car to discover the vehicle next to mine sitting forlornly on its axles, all four wheels having been stolen.

It's been almost two weeks, I thought. *What if the Jeep doesn't start after all this time? What if someone has stolen* my *wheels or siphoned my gas?*

However, my worry was unfounded. The Jeep was just as we had left it eleven days before. The engine fired up immediately, and I drove down the hill to where Sue stood talking to the two women who had been part of the group at the dock. Their canoes and two additional backpacks lay by ours. I assumed the men had returned to the dock for the rest of their gear.

Sue continued to chat with the women while I loaded our packs into the Jeep, positioned the canoe on the car-top racks, and tied it down. When she realized I was ready to go, she left the group in a chorus of good-byes and slid into the passenger seat.

"Thanks for all the help," I groused, starting the Jeep.

"Oh, did you need some help? Sorry," she grinned. "But we were having a really interesting conversation. Did you know I'm a celebrity on the circuit?"

"Oh, really?" I asked, as I pulled from the shoulder of the road.

"It seems I am," she laughed. "When I introduced myself as Sue, one of them asked if I was the Sue who got bonked on the head with a pack. When I said I was, they told me they'd been hearing about me all along the way. People kept telling them how brave I was to keep going on the trip and how good-spirited I took everything."

"*Bonked?* Is that the word they used?"

"No, that's the word *I* use. I think they said something like 'Are you the poor lady whose husband dropped a pack on her head?'"

"I *thought* they threw me some cold looks," I observed.

"Well, it *is* a little bit of a *Beauty and the Beast* story. And since I'm the beauty, I guess that makes you the . . ."

"Yeah, yeah, I know. I'm the beast."

"But you're a sweetheart beast," she cooed, leaning over to pat me on the thigh.

*　　*　　*

After checking out at the Registration Center, we were driving through the parking lot on our way to the exit road when Sue suddenly yelled, "Stop! Stop!"

"What is it?" I answered, slamming on the brakes, and instinctively checking the rearview mirror for the remains of a squirrel or some other hapless creature I had just squashed.

"Speaking of beasts," she said, "look over there." She pointed to a vehicle parked on our right. The forest-green Land Rover, layered with grime, looked like a homemade tank with its iron grillwork welded to the sides and top. Iron-screened compartments above the back wheel wells held gas cans locked into place with heavy chains and padlocks. A knobby spare tire was bolted to the back of the rig. Another rested on top of the Land Rover, it, too, chained and padlocked.

"That's *The Beast*, isn't it?" Sue bubbled.

"I'm sure it is," I agreed. "Albin and Christina must still be on the circuit."

"Do we have a plastic bag handy?" Sue asked, opening the glove compartment and rummaging through it.

"There're a couple in the day pack. Why?"

"Because," she explained, pulling out a writing pad and pen, "I'm going to break your mountain-man rule and leave them a note with our phone number and address. That way we might be able to stay in touch."

"Okay, but why the plastic bag?"

"I assume *The Beast* is locked. So I'm going to have to leave the note under the windshield wiper. That's why I'm putting it in the bag. If it rains, they won't find some soggy mess that looks like a Jackson Pollock original."

"Good thinking," I agreed.

CHAMPAGNE AND FUTURE PLANS

"You were right," Sue smiled, breaking apart a buttery piece of garlic bread. "You said when we got back here, I'd be craving a steak, fresh salad, baked potato—the whole works. Frankly, I didn't believe you. I mean, it's such a caveman dinner. But I think I can truly say this is one of the best meals I've ever had.

We were sitting in the steakhouse in Quesnel where we had eaten the night before we set out on the circuit. I watched Sue over the candle-lit table. She was in such high spirits, obviously happy to be back in civilization.

I marveled at how cleverly she had folded a scarf into something resembling a headband and used it to cover the shaved area of her head. Her face was tan from eleven days in the weather, a tan that emphasized the turquoise blue of her eyes. A flowered blouse seemed so feminine after days of seeing her in camp shirts over cargo pants.

"Why are you studying me like that?" she smiled.

"I was just thinking how well you clean up."

"Well, I could say the same about you. I'd almost forgotten what you look like without whiskers."

We were silent for a few moments before Sue commented, "Anyway, it was a great trip."

"Really? It wasn't too hard, then?"

"Oh, it was hard," she replied. "Much harder than I expected in spite of all your warnings. I have to confess that today when we were paddling down Bowron Lake, I was so exhausted. But now, after a shower, a nap on a soft bed, the opportunity to put on a little makeup—well, I'm a new woman."

"You did so well, Babes. I'm proud of you."

"Oh, I've been putting on makeup for years."

"No, I mean on the circuit. You did so well on the circuit."

"I knew what you meant," she smiled. "And the next time we do the trip, it'll be even better because I'll know what to expect."

"Next time? There's going to be a next time?"

"Of course, there is." After a pause, she asked, "Isn't there? I mean, you've been coming up here off and on for what—fourteen, fifteen years? I just assumed you'd be back. And you're not coming without me."

I leaned forward. "You don't know how relieved that makes me, Babes. I figured once would be enough for you."

"Oh, I'm a person of many surprises," she laughed.

"Yes, you are." I waited a beat and then offered, "Remember what Stan said last night? About if we came back next year at this time, we'd have a good chance of running into them? Maybe we ought to think about it."

"Next year? You're thinking next year? I thought you always took a couple of years off between trips. Next year seems a little soon doesn't it?" She looked away as she waited for my answer.

"You're right," I agreed. "Next year would be way too soon."

I reached to the silver ice bucket beside the table, lifted the dripping champagne bottle, and topped off our glasses. "So if not Bowron Lakes, how about Maui next summer?"

"Maui?" she smiled. "You want to go back to Maui next year?"

"Sure. You don't have any qualms about going to Maui two years in a row, do you?"

"No," she laughed, "I don't. Maui next summer would be wonderful."

"All right, then." I lifted my glass. "To Maui."

Sue started to lift her glass and then set it down. "No," she shook her head. She raised the glass again and held it toward me. "To Bowron."

I reached across the table, and lightly touched my glass to hers. "Yes," I smiled. "To Bowron."

EPILOGUE

Sue and I never returned to Bowron Lakes. And, maybe, not going back was for the best. While other trips might have offered different challenges and different discoveries, they could also have been anticlimactic, overshadowed by Sue's first wilderness adventure.

After all, this was Sue's trip. I was simply along for the ride. At one point on the circuit, she remarked that no one in her family would ever believe she was capable of facing such challenges. I suspect if Sue had really understood the demands of a wilderness experience when we were planning the trip, she would have agreed with her family. But she *did* handle the challenges. She handled them with courage, good humor, and a wealth of strength—both physical and mental—that she had never recognized in herself. This wasn't growth. She didn't develop these attributes as we went along. This was self-realization. She could do what people all her life had convinced her she could not do. Added to this self-discovery were her unfailing optimism, love of people, and ability to keep my ego in check. The foundation of our lives together was established on this trip around the Bowron Lakes.

* * *

People who have paddled the circuit in the last few years may have trouble finding themselves in this narrative. In fact-checking my memory, I discovered the Park Service has been busy making the trip easier for travelers.

Sue and I made three trips over each portage, first to carry the canoe and lighter gear and then a return for the packs. Today's visitors make a single trip on each portage. They rent canoe carts, wheeled contraptions that are pushed and pulled along the trails. They can load most of their gear into the canoes, put extras in a light backpack, and be on their way. Of course, the trails needed to be improved for these carts. They've been widened, graded, and made more wheel-friendly with sand and gravel.

Probably no one doing the trip today knows Babcock Creek was once Three Mile Creek—or even cares, for that matter. Now it's simply a little stream along a new portage trail. Sue and I agree that lining Three Mile Creek was one of our best times on the circuit. Wading shallow water while pulling along an obedient canoe is a delightful experience, one of the best ways to appreciate a canoe's versatility. But today canoeists no longer line the creek. I'd like to think the decision to build an additional portage trail was based upon a need to protect the fragility of the creek and its beaver dams. However, I can't help wondering if the trail isn't really there for the convenience of wheeled transportation.

Most of the platform bear caches in the trees are gone. Only a couple have been preserved as antique oddities for today's travelers. Now each campsite has a large metal box with a bear-proof latch. This sounds like an excellent improvement. I suspect no husband has yet to climb to the top of one of these boxes and drop a pack on his wife's head.

The campgrounds have also been upgraded. More campsites have been added, and at least four covered picnic shelters have been constructed along the way, each with a wood stove, picnic tables, and concrete floor.

I must admit I'm put off by these improvements. Graded trails to accommodate canoe carts, stoves, picnic tables, and concrete floors? Isn't the park becoming a little too civilized?

I know the more comfortable campers are, the less likely they'll harm the environment by attempting to make their own improvements. Nevertheless, I believe the majority of people coming to the Bowron Lakes are there for a wilderness experience. Improvements can go only so far before the wild has been taken out of the wilderness.

*　　*　　*

Christina and Albin *did* contact us after finding Sue's note on *The Beast.* We exchanged letters, photographs, and, yes, Christmas cards, giving Sue an "I-told-you-so" moment.

As for that picture of the two of us on the canoe float at the end of the trip, it is one of my favorites. Sue and I have traveled the world in the twenty-three years since we paddled the Bowron Lake circuit. And everywhere we've gone, we've performed the obligatory camera exchange with others. We have pictures of ourselves before a glacier in Iceland, on a mountain ledge above a Norwegian fjord, on the balcony of Hitler's Eagle's Nest, at the Acropolis in Athens, before the Blue Mosque in Istanbul, alongside a Crusaders' castle on the denuded hills of Malta, and on the battlements of Dracula's castle in Transylvania.

On the other side of the world, the cameras have caught us on a ferry in the Hong Kong harbor, atop the Great Wall of China, near the DMZ in Korea, on the grounds of a Buddhist temple near Kyoto, and wading a palm-shaded lagoon in the Cook Islands of the South Pacific.

However, my favorite is this photograph of two people in crumpled, stained camping clothes, standing by their canoe on a lakeside dock under dark, cloudy skies. Two people who began a wilderness adventure as newlyweds and ended it as best friends for life.

Best friends for life

Edwards Brothers,Inc!
Thorofare, NJ 08086
01 Aug, 2010
BA2010213